TROUBLESHOOTING
OLD CARS
BY RON BISHOP

TAB BOOKS Inc.
BLUE RIDGE SUMMIT, PA. 17214

FIRST EDITION

FIRST PRINTING

Copyright © 1982 by TAB BOOKS Inc.

Printed in the United States of America

Library of Congress Cataloging in Publication Data

Bishop, Ron, 1937-
    Troubleshooting old cars.

    Includes index.
    1. Automobiles—Maintenance and repair.
I. Title.
TL152.B384   1982   629.28'722   82-5924
ISBN 0-8306-3075-9   AACR2
ISBN 0-8306-2075-3 (pbk.)

Contents

Introduction

Troubleshooting is a process of elimination to establish the facts, find out whether or not a suspected trouble actually exists, and to then track down the source in a logical manner.

I recommend that you do not make any adjustments or repairs until a complete analysis of the trouble is complete and that you are positive the source of the trouble has been located. Working slovenly, trying this and that, while hoping to stumble on the cause of trouble could result in changing the effect of the trouble and thereby entirely disguise the actual cause of the trouble.

Under some special circumstances, certain possible causes of erratic operation of failure of a unit could result from several kinds of trouble. There are often many reasons for similar automotive troubles. Therefore, it would be wise to consider the entire listing under each major trouble. Engine noises, lubrication, carburetion, ignition troubles and so on, can be interpreted in so many ways that full benefit from this analysis is not obtained unless the entire listing under each heading is perused.

The key ingredient is PMC: be patient, work methodically and meticulously and above all, keep your cool. Troubleshooting an old car is an art that can only be developed with practice. This book will guide you in the right direction.

Acknowledgments

As in any work of this type, a vast number of sources has been consulted. I hope the unintentional omission of credit to any individual, organization, company, or corporation will be excused. Acknowledgment is hereby expressed to the automotive industry in general for its generous cooperation, antique auto hobbyists, and to all my friends who helped me compile this information. Special thanks to Bill Cannon, Henry Miller, Sig Caswell, Chuck Groninga, Tom Hutchinson, Lester Goetz, and John Waugh who were all instrumental in the development of this book.

ENGINE

Lack of Power, Speed, and Acceleration

1—Grade of fuel not suited to engine.
2—Accelerator does not open throttle fully.
3—Carbon in cylinders (on valves and on valve seats).
4—Excessive friction due to tight engine bearings.
5—Clearance between cylinders and pistons is too small.
6—Car does not roll free due to excessive friction, dragging brakes, or underinflated tires.
7—Engine not properly tuned. *See* Carburetor and Ignition.
8—Breaker points not synchronized.
9—Worn breaker points or breaker point cam.
10—Automatic spark control inoperative.
11—Valve clearance not properly adjusted.
12—Unequal compression in cylinders.
13—Poor compression.
14—Mixture too rich or too lean.
15—Air leaks at manifold joints, carburetor, or vacuum-operated accessories.
16—Carburetor bypass valve stuck in the closed position.
17—Heat setting incorrect for the grade of fuel being used.
18—Automatic heat control sticking or improper adjustment of thermostat.
19—Excessive back pressure in muffler.
20—Muffler/tail pipe jammed against inner muffler baffle.
21—Clutch slipping (*See* Clutch).
22—Air cleaner clogged causing rich mixture and smoky exhaust.
23—*See also* Carburetor, Ignition, Engine Misfires, and Engine Overheats.

Hard-Starting Engine

1—Mixture too rich or too lean.
2—Incorrect use of manual choke.
3—Engine flooded due to defective or sticking automatic choke control, choke valve distorted by backfire, pumping accelerator pedal.
4—Carburetor flooding.
5—Fuel level in float chamber low.
6—Water seeping into cylinders.
7—Water or dirt in fuel.
8—Push rods not properly adjusted.
9—Valve stem guides worn (especially intake guides).
10—Weak valve springs.
11—Leak at the intake manifold or carburetor.

12—Poor compression due to poor mechanical condition of the engine or poor seating valves.
13—Slow cranking of engine.
14—Weak or late ignition.
15—Battery weak or discharged.
16—Loose or corroded battery terminals.
17—Poor battery ground connection.
18—Loose breaker points.
19—Breaker points sticking or dirty.
20—Loose breaker arm post.
21—Spark plug electrodes too far apart.
22—Poor distributor ground.
23—Partially shorted or open Electrolock to distributor cable.
24—Rotor gap in distributor too large or moisture in gap.
25—Loose resistance unit on coil.
26—Poor mechanical condition of distributor or drive.
27—Loose connections between switch and distributor.
28—Loose connection between switch and battery.

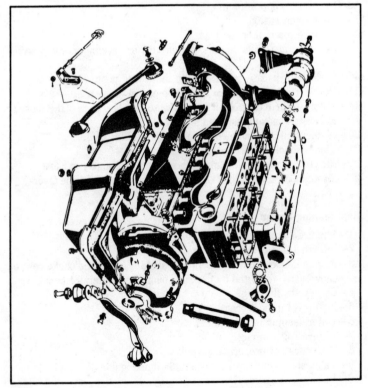

Engine.

29—Generator charging rate too high causing pitting of breaker points.
30—High resistance in charging circuit causes low voltage at ignition coil.
31—Poor ground between engine and chassis.

Engine Will Not Start

1—Water in carburetor (frozen shutting off fuel).
2—Throttle inoperative.
3—Cylinders flooded with raw fuel.
4—Poor compression.
5—Timing chain broken (engine out of time).
6—Timing gear key sheared.
7—Foreign matter between flywheel gear and housing.
8—Starter gear stripped.
9—Starter pinion jammed.
10—Starter drive gummed with oil.
11—Broken Bendix drive spring.
12—Starter bearings seized.
13—Battery weak or completely discharged.
14—Battery connections loose or corroded; poor ground connection.
15—Starter switch does not make contact.
16—Breaker arm stuck open.
17—Foreign matter between breaker points.
18—Generator drive gear loose on shaft affecting distributor drive.
19—Generator armature shaft broken affecting distributor drive.
20—Distributor drive gear loose, broken, or out of mesh.
21—Coil burnt out, damp, or not properly grounded.
22—Loose high-tension wire from distributor to coil.
23—Water on high-tension coil terminal.
24—Distributor wires not in place.
25—Ignition switch safety button out (when employed).
26—Inoperative fuel pump.
27—Faulty ignition switch; switch wire disconnected or loose.
28—Water leak in cylinders.
29—Engine oil congealed at low temperatures.
30—Transmission gears in mesh and brakes "on."
31—*See also* Carburetor, Electrical System, Spark Plugs, Ignition, and Starting Motor.

Engine Slows Down Intermittently and Regains Speed

1—Air leaks in vacuum spark control line.
2—Poor distributor ground.
3—Clogged exhaust (try a new muffler).
4—Poor ground at the battery.
5—Poor engine ground (rubber-mounted engine).
6—Soft fuel hose (collapses under suction).

Engine Stalls on Curves

1—Loose baffle plate in gasoline tank obstructing fuel flow.

Bucking

1—Make sure the engine is properly tuned so it will function perfectly at low speed.
2—Automatic choke not opening quick enough (causing loading).
3—Timing chain not properly adjusted or worn. This affects the timing of the engine.
4—Valves sticking in the valve guide.
5—Air leaks through valve guides (leaning out mixture at low speeds).
6—*See also* Excessive Backlash under Clutch, Transmission, Rear Axle, and Universal Joints.

Backlash is usually called *bucking*. This condition is usually noticeable at "lazying" or "floating" speed when the momentum of the vehicle and crankshaft fail to synchronize.

Engine Stalls

1—Ignition failure.
2—Improper carburetor adjustment.
3—High fuel pump pressure.
4—A small particle or a flake of solder can clog the fuel pipe in the gasoline tank.
5—Fuel level in carburetor too high.

Engine Will Not Idle

1—Poor ignition.
2—Improper carburetor adjustment.
3—Gas spreader in intake manifold bent out of shape or improperly installed.
4—Sticking valves.
5—Poor compression.
6—Spark plug gaps too narrow.
7—Ignition timed too early.

Engine Will Idle but Will Not Accelerate

1—Clogged muffler or obstructed exhaust line causing excessive back pressure.
2—*See also* Ignition System, Carburetor, and Fuel System.

Poor Idling

1—Engine stiff, will not idle well until "broken-in".
2—*See also* Engine Misfires, Ignition System and Carburetor.

Engine Starts Hard when Hot

1—Fuel boiling in the float chamber forces fuel out of the jets into manifold to flood the engine.
2—Percolation in carburetor.
3—Anti-percolator valve fails to open.
4—Loose metering or defective discharge jets in the carburetor.
5—Defective jet gaskets in the carburetor.
6—High fuel level.

Engine Fires with Switch "Off"

1—Defective switch; does not open circuit.
2—Dirty spark plugs or cracked insulators.
3—Overheated spark plugs.
4—Engine idling too fast due to sticking condition in throttle or accelerator linkage.
5—Engine idling too fast due to maladjustment of hand throttle control linkage.
6—Engine idling too fast due to sticking accelerator pump.
7—*See also* Engine Misfires, Ignition System, and Carburetor.

Overheating

1—*See* Engine Overheats.

Misfiring

1—*See* Engine Misfires.

Compression

1—Low compression, not brought up to normal by oil seal, might be due to the valve not seating or because of a gasket leak. The gasket might be blown between adjacent cylinders or foreign material might prevent proper seating. A gasket leak can be to water jackets. In such a case there will be water in cylinders and in the oil, and a low water level in the radiator. A gasket blow to the outside will be heard.
2—High compression. More than 10 pounds over normal indicates excessive carbon has changed compression ratio.

Weak Compression

1—Leaky spark plug gaskets or broken insulators.
2—Leaky cylinder head gasket.
3—Cylinder walls out-of-round or tapered excessively.
4—Scored pistons or cylinder walls.
5—Loose pistons.
6—Broken piston rings.
7—Rings fouled (sticking in the piston groove).
8—Compression ring stuck in the cylinder head on sleeve-valve engines.

5

9—Cracked piston head.
10—Cracked cylinder head.
11—Push rod clearance too small (holding valves open).
12—Valves not seating, sticking, or warped (poor valve seats).
13—Weak valve springs.
14—Broken valve spring retainer.
15—Use of the wrong kind of oil; oil too thin or excessively diluted.
16—Idling mixture too lean.

Cylinders Scored

1—Engine overheating.
2—Lack of lubrication.
3—Broken or loose piston pin.
4—Connecting rod out-of-alignment.
5—Piston out-of-round or tight.
6—*See also* Engine Overheats and Engine Lubrication.

Cylinders Carboned

1—Mixture too rich.
2—Over lubrication.
3—Pistons, rings, or cylinders worn excessively.
4—Pistons, rings, or cylinders scored.
5—Ignition timed late. This encourages carbon formation and reduces power.
6—*See also* Carburetor and Engine Lubrication.

Engine Stiff

1—Faulty lubrication.
2—Engine oil congealed.
3—Cylinders and pistons scored.
4—Tight pistons.
5—Piston pin seized.
6—Tight engine bearings.
7—Tight timing gears or front end drive.
8—*See also* Engine Lubrication.

Valves Sticking

1—Valve springs weak or broken.
2—Valve stem or guide worn. Exhaust worn and carboned.
3—Valve stem and guide overheated.
4—Valve stem bent.
5—Gum in fuel.

Valve Spring Breakage

1—Spring cocked (not properly assembled correctly).

2—Spring ends not parallel and square with axis.
3—Shimmy or flutter at high speeds.
4—Damper not properly assembled.
5—Sludge between coils formed in valve compartment due to overoiling, excessive heat, or improper ventilation.
6—Moisture in valve compartment combined with heat crystalizes spring material.

Valve Tappet Clearance Lost

1—Valve guide and valve seat not concentric.
2—End of valve stem not true with stem axis.
3—Tappet adjusting screw head not true altering clearance as tappet rotates.
4—Tappet guides worn permitting misalignment of tappets due to cam thrust.
5—Cam surface of tappet not true.
6—Valves stretching.
7—Tappet roller worn eccentric.
8—Tappet roller pin worn eccentric.
9—Rocker arm arc contacting valve not true.
10—Rocker arm shaft bearing worn permitting shaft to float and alter clearance.

Valves Require Frequent Reconditioning

1—Push rods adjusted with too little clearance.
2—Valve stems, push rods, or rocker arms sticking.
3—Valve guides and valve seats not concentric.
4—Valve springs weak.

Valves Burn

1—Valves stick open.
2—Push rods stick holding valves open.
3—Valve seat not concentric with guide.
4—Valve stem bent holding valve open.
5—Inferior valve material.
6—Engine overheating.
7—Valve seats too narrow.
8—Lack of push rod clearance, valves held open.
9—Lack of clearance between valve stem and guide.
10—Weak valve springs.

Main Bearing Failure

1—Lack of lubrication.
2—Fitted with too little clearance.
3—Poor seating of bearing shell in its mounting.

4—Burrs or projecting dowel prevent proper seating of bearing in its mounting.

5—Broken bond between metal and shell.

6—Poor alignment.

7—Bearing journal tapered or out-of-round.

8—Improperly assembled (shell turned obstructing oil holes).

9—Crankshaft weak (excessive deflection of shaft overloading the bearings).

10—Oil and bearing temperatures too high.

11—Lack of sufficient end clearance causing seizure.

12—Oil line obstructed.

13—Bearing journals rough.

Connecting Rod Bearing Failure

1—Bearing adjusted (not round). Load carried on small bearing surface also permitting escape of oil.

2—Misalignment of connecting rod.

3—Lack of sufficient end clearance.

4—Overheating due to damaged side thrust surfaces of rod and cap.

5—Excessive out-of-roundness of crankpin journals.

6—Incorrect assembly of rod and bearing.

7—*See also* Main Bearing Failure.

Cylinder Reconditioning Failure

1—Cylinder bores not in alignment with crankshaft.

2—Pistons not in alignment with cylinder bores.

3—Misaligned connecting rods or piston pins.

4—Poorly fit or tight-fitting piston pins.

5—Cylinder bore not true or parallel throughout length.

6—Improper piston clearance.

7—Ring gap clearance too small causing unequal and excessive cylinder wall pressure.

8—Cylinder warpage or distortion.

9—Slovenly tightening of cylinder head (causing distortion).

10—Warped valve seats distorting cylinder bore.

11—Cylinder walls lack smoothness and wear rapidly.

12—Overheating and uneven cooling.

13—Lack of or ineffective lubrication.

14—Watery, dirty, diluted, or inferior oil being used.

15—Failure to remove abrasive dust and thoroughly wash cylinder bore.

16—Scale and sediment in water jackets causing uneven cooling and local hot spots.

17—Poor ignition or faulty carburetor adjustment.

18—Excessive use of manually controlled choke by driver or sticking automatic choke.

Engine Rough

1—Clutch driven disc or pressure plate out of balance. This must be held within ¼ of an ounce.

Water in Combustion Chamber

1—Cylinder head gasket leaking.
2—Cylinder head studs or bolts loose.
3—Cracked water jacket.
4—Sand hole in casting.

Water Leaking at Exhaust in Cylinder

1—Loose cylinder head.
2—Leaking cylinder head gasket.
3—Cracked water jacket.
4—Cracked valve seat.

Cylinder Head or Block Cracked

1—Water in water jackets frozen.
2—Cylinder head bolts or studs not tightened evenly.
3—Aluminum-head bolts or studs tightened while engine is hot.

Note: In either of the above three cases, and with weak compression, any loss of compression to the cooling system will be indicated by bubbles in the cooling water (visible through radiator filler neck) if the engine is at normal operating temperature and then cranked by hand with ignition "off."

Engine Out-of-Alignment

1—Loose hold-down bolts.
2—Frame or cross-member rivets loose.
3—Engine improperly aligned at assembly.
4—Deterioration of rubber parts in engine mounting.

Smoky Exhaust

1—Oil level too high (splash system).
2—Oil pressure too high.
3—Oil too thin.
4—Oil pumping. *See* Engine Lubrication.
5—Improper top oilers.
6—Mixture too rich.
7—*See also* Engine Lubrication. Black smoke indicates the mixture is too rich. Blue smoke indicates overlubrication.

Excessive Fuel Consumption (low MPG)

1—*See* Carburetor, Fuel System, Ignition System, and Spark Plugs.

Engine Hesitates at High Speed

1—Defective spark plugs or plug gaps not properly adjusted.
2—Carburetor jets partially clogged.
3—Carburetor adjustment set too lean.
4—Check ignition system for proper timing, breaker point gap, condition of points, wear in distributor parts, and breaker point synchronism.
5—Vacuum advance sticking to retard normal centrifugal advance of spark.
6—*See also* Carburetor, Ignition System, and Spark Plugs.

Torsional Vibration

1—Improper functioning of vibration damper due to improper assembly, improper adjustment (when adjustable), stuck or inoperative damper, and damper loose on crankshaft.
2—Excessive backlash in front-end drive.
3—Excessive front camshaft bearing clearance.
4—Excessive front main bearing clearance.
5—Engine slightly loose in mountings.
6—Eccentric timing gear.
7—Timing gears loose on their shafts.

High Speed Vibration

1—Unequal compression of engine cylinders.
2—Distributor points not synchronized.
3—Misfiring at high speed.
4—Incorrect adjustment of rubber engine mountings.
5—Unbalanced fan or loose fan blades.
6—Unbalanced flywheel.
7—Unbalanced clutch assembly.
8—Variation in weight of reciprocating parts.
9—Engine mountings loose.
10—Unbalanced or sprung crankshaft.
11—Excessive engine frictional resistance due to insufficient internal clearances, scored pistons, or use of too heavy engine oil.

Engine Warms Up Sluggishly

1—Carbon in the intake manifold heat riser section.

Engine Cuts Out at High Speed

1—Manifold heat control valve stuck in closed or partially closed position.

Poor Acceleration with Engine Warm

1—Carbon in intake manifold heat riser.

Exhaust Manifold Heats Excessively

1—Manifold heat control valve stuck in closed or partially closed position.

ENGINE MISFIRES

Engine Misfires at All Speeds

1—Defective spark plugs.
2—Irregular ignition.
3—Oil pumping (fouled spark plugs).
4—Battery partially discharged.
5—Battery connection loose, corroded, or poorly grounded.
6—Wire connections at the distributor or coil are loose or corroded.
7—Cracked or dirty coil head.
8—Poor distributor ground.
9—Poor coil. Ground when necessary.
10—Poor engine ground (with rubber engine mounting).
11—Improper carburetor adjustment.
12—Foreign substance in fuel.
13—Water in float chamber.
14—Cracked heat riser (exhaust diluting mixture same as an air leak).
15—Low test or dirty gasoline.
16—Improper adjustment of choke mechanism.
17—Vacuum tank flooding.
18—Poor compression.
19—Weak valve springs.
20—Valves holding open.
21—Defective cylinder head gasket.
22—Broken cam on camshaft.
23—Air leaks in intake system.
24—Leak in windshield wiper connection diluting mixture.
25—Combination fuel and vacuum pump (defective vacuum pump diaphragm).
26—*See also* Engine Lubrication, Carburetor, Fuel System, and Ignition System.

Engine Misfires at High Speed

1—Carburetor adjusted too lean or too rich.
2—Vacuum tank starved.
3—Obstructed gasoline line.
4—Defective spark plugs.
5—Oil fouling spark plugs.
6—Weak ignition.
7—Poorly grounded distributor, battery, or coil.
8—Poor ground for a rubber-mounted engine.
9—Weak coil.

10—Excessive carbon in cylinders.
11—Valves not properly timed.
12—Valve stems bent, valves sticking or not seating, weak valve springs.
13—Broken inner valve spring.
14—Push rod bushing loose.
15—Bent push rods on overhead valve engine.
16—Valve stems not adjusted for clearance at engine operating temperature.
17—Air leaks effective at high speeds only.
18—Use of chemically treated fuel causing deposits to form on spark plug insulator.
19—Fuel pump not holding pressure consistently.
20—Gasoline tank cap not properly vented.
21—High opening thermostat in cooling system causes vapor lock with certain grades of fuel.
22—Broken pigtail wire inside insulation in connection between coil wire terminal and contact point arm.
23—*See also* Carburetor, Spark Plugs, Fuel System, and Ignition System.

Engine Misfires at Low Speed on Pull

1—Weak compression.
2—Air leaks at the intake manifold.
3—Air leaks at the carburetor flange or throttle shaft.
4—Imperfect fuel mixture.
5—Insufficient heat on carburetor.
6—Excessive carbon in cylinders.
7—Defective cylinder head gasket.
8—Weak or broken valve springs.
9—Valves timed too early.
10—Valves not seating properly.
11—Worn valve stems or guides.
12—Push rods adjusted with too little clearance.
13—Poor ignition.
14—Defective spark plugs.
15—Fouled spark plugs.
16—Use of chemically treated fuel causing deposit to form on the spark plug insulator.
17—Battery weak. Loose or corroded terminals. Poor battery ground.
18—Vacuum too low to raise fuel to the vacuum tank.
19—*See also* Carburetor, Ignition System, Spark Plugs, Compression, and Engine Lubrication.

Engine Misfires at Low Speed Idling

1—Defective spark plugs.
2—Oil fouling spark plugs.
3—Spark advanced too far.

4—Battery weak.

5—Loose or corroded battery terminals.

6—Poor ground for battery.

7—Poor distributor ground.

8—Poor coil ground when necessary.

9—Poor engine ground (rubber mounting).

10—Engine not properly tuned for idling.

11—Poor or uneven compression.

12—Weak coil.

13—Too little clearance at push rods (valves do not close).

14—Valves not seating properly.

15—Poor valve seats.

16—Weak valve springs.

17—Cylinder head loose.

18—Cracked cylinder head or cylinder block.

19—Air leaks at the intake manifold or carburetor.

20—Mixture too rich or too lean.

21—Carburetor low-speed jet is clogged.

22—Distributor gap being altered when vacuum spark control is active.

23—Leaking windshield wiper connection or line.

24—*See also* Spark Plugs, Ignition System, Carburetor, Fuel System, Compression, and Engine Lubrication.

Engine Misses or Cuts Out at Definite Speed

1—Certain conditions causing shorting of primary current at cutting-out speed. Check insulation of exposed primary wiring for defective insulation.

Engine Misfires on One Cylinder

1—Usually due to a weak spark at the spark plug and can also be caused by a cracked distributor cap or shorting in the distributor cap. Spark shorting to the next cylinder in the firing sequence.

2—Cracked valve seat.

3—Sticking valve.

Regular Misfiring Same Bank of Cylinders

1—Heat riser cracked or burned through.

2—Improper wiring of the distributor to the spark plugs.

Note: Engine performance is dependent upon proper ignition, carburetion, and compression. Only a properly tuned engine can give smooth idling and snappy getaway. *See* Engine Test with Vacuum Gauge and Ignition Defects on Test Stand.

Wandering Miss in Engine

1—Creeping breaker arm causing points to slide along rather than break clearly.

2—Heat riser burnt through irregularly diluting mixture with exhaust gas.

3—Obstruction in manifold that has loosened and is being lifted to hold a valve open when it should be seated.

4—Valve sticking (don't be misled by vacuum and compression checking OK).

5—Weak valve springs.

6—Back pressure in muffler or exhaust line (line or muffler clogged or loose baffle in muffler).

7—Automatic spark advance inoperative or sticking.

8—Vacuum advance sticking.

9—Sticking or tightly fitted piston rings.

10—Obstruction in fuel tank shutting off or restricting fuel flow.

11—Floating particles in cooling system prevent thermostat from functioning.

ENGINE NOISES

Engine noise under various operating conditions is a very difficult subject to break down and then reclassify each particular noise for a complete analysis of all cases. While space does not permit listing every definition or description, these various noises have been covered under major classifications to simplify diagnosis. Use a listening rod or stethoscope to determine the approximate location of the noise. Also check by means of shorting out the plugs when conditions permit. Engine noise in general results from mechanical conditions that can be understood. Remedies should be obvious in all cases.

Pronounced Knock in an Engine Under Pull

1—Excessive carbon in combustion chambers.

2—Loose connecting rod bearings.

3—Main bearing worn or loose.

4—Main or connecting rod bearing burned out.

5—Loose flywheel.

6—Piston rings worn, loose, or broken.

7—Loose piston. Worn or warped cylinder walls.

8—Main bearing dowel pins loose.

9—Foreign substance between the teeth of timing gears.

10—Broken piston pin.

11—End play in the crankshaft.

12—Vapor lock. *See* carburetor.

13—Sleeve rod interference on sleeve valve engines.

14—Harmonic balancer loose on crankshaft.

15—Standard-size bearing used on reconditioned shaft that is undersize.

Dull Pound

1—Engine mounting loose.

Dull Thump when Engine Is Idling

1—Excessive end play in crankshaft.
2—Loose flywheel.
3—Bearing burned out.
4—Sticking valve or bent valve stem.
5—Worn camshaft bearings.
6—Generator end play.

Piston Slap

1—Loose pistons.
2—Cylinder walls scored or worn.
3—Connecting rod out of alignment.

Sharp Click or Knock in Engine

1—Excessive carbon in cylinders.
2—Ignition set early.
3—Carburetor adjustment too lean.
4—Improperly seated rocker arm on overhead valve engine.
5—Broken fan bearing.
6—Pistons too loose. *See* Piston Slap.
7—Loose piston pin.
8—Broken valve spring.
9—Push rod clearance too great.
10—Broken piston ring.
11—Ring click due to new ring striking ridge worn in cylinder.
12—Loose piston pin clamp screw.
13—Fan blades striking some obstacle.
14—Worn valve guides cause a knock.

Knock in One Cylinder

1—Due to wrong installation of connecting rod
2—*See* Pronounced Knock in Engine Under Pull, Piston Slap, and Rap in Engine When Idling.

Loud Metallic Rattle

1—Broken piston.
2—Loose fan bracket.

Metallic Rattle while Accelerating

1—Loose muffler shells or baffles.

Rap in Engine at High Speed

1—Loose fan belt (noise similar to spark rap at high speed).

Spark Knock at Wide-Open Throttle
1—Breaker plate sticking in advanced position.

Bump or Thud at Front End of Engine at Low Engine Speed
1—Loose vibration damper.

Knock at Normal Driving Speed (35 mph)
1—Camshaft fiber gear loose on its hub.

Chattering Noise in Water Pump
1—Porous pump shaft bushings not absorbing oil.

Rap in Engine when Idling
1—Connecting rod out of alignment. Upper end whipping against piston pin boss or lower end whipping sideways on crankshaft.
2—Loose piston pin.
3—Broken piston ring.
4—Piston inner ring weak or broken.
5—Excessive end play in crankshaft.
6—Cams on camshaft scored or worn.
7—Foreign substance in generator coupling.
8—Oil pressure too high causing pressure knock.
9—Junk ring loose in head (sleeve-valve engines).
10—Sleeve rods loose or sprung (sleeve-valve engines).
11—Compression rings warped allowing lower edge to spring into sleeve port (sleeve-valve engines).
12—Excessive end play in eccentric shaft (sleeve-valve engines).

Noisy Push Rods or Valve Lifters
1—Too much lifter or push rod clearance.
2—Push rods or lifters not rotating properly causing excessive wear of cam contact surface.
3—Push rods or lifters worn or scored at cam surface.
4—Worn or out-of-round push rod or lifter stem.
5—Worn push rod or lifter guide, broken or improperly assembled.
6—Cams on camshaft worn or scored.
7—Bent push rods on overhead valve engines.
8—Rocker arms dry on overhead valve engines.
9—Push rod or lifter adjusting screw head worn changing valve clearance.
10—Valve stem surface contacting push rod or lifter worn.
11—Push rod or lifter cluster bracket loose or out of alignment.
12—Uneven wear of push rod or lifter cam surfaces.
13—Weak valve springs.

Automatic Lash Tappet Noise

1—Air in oil due to too high oil level in crankcase.
2—Dirt in mechanism.
3—Oil lead to tappet clogged.

Valve Noise Similar to Loose Tappet, Push Rod, or Lifter

1—Dry push rod or lifter.
2—Rocker arms do not get sufficient lubrication on overhead valve engines.
3—Excessive wear of rocker arms on overhead valve engines.
4—Lack of clearance between rocker arm and valve spring retainer on overhead valve engines.
5—Worn push rod or lifter; scored cam surface.
6—Valve spring cocked (not concentric with valve stem).
7—Valve spring surge or shimmy.
8—Springs not properly assembled (installed bottom side up).
9—Half of spring coils in vertical plane set (weak).
10—Valve spring dampers ineffective.
11—Valve sticking in guides.
12—Spring coils touching when valve is open.

Noise in Front End Drive

1—Gears or sprockets worn; chain worn.
2—Gears or sprockets loose on their shafts.
3—Gears or sprockets not running true on their shafts or excessive end play in shafts.
4—Sprung fan shaft or distributor drive shaft. Excessive end play in either shaft.
5—Fan blades setting up vibration.
6—Camshaft thrust plunger rough and tapping timing gear cover.
7—Oil pan not properly positioned. Gear or sprocket teeth striking gasket.
8—Fan bearings dry.
9—Camshaft thrust plunger spring broken.
10—Camshaft bearings loose in crankcase.
11—Fan belt slipping.
12—Camshaft sprocket loose on camshaft.

Timing Chain Noise

1—Chain excessively worn.
2—Chain not properly adjusted; too tight or too much slack.
3—Chain not being properly lubricated.
4—Sprockets out of alignment.
5—Generator out of alignment when chain driven.
6—Chain etched by acid formed in lubricating oil.
7—Generator charging rate too high (overloading the chain).

Timing Gears Noisy

1—One or more gears worn.
2—Idler stud worn.
3—Idler gear loose.
4—Generator out of alignment when gear driven.
5—Idler gear seized on stud.
6—Gears meshed without backlash.
7—Gears meshed with too much backlash.
8—Front camshaft bearing worn.
9—Broken tooth on gear.
10—Crankshaft sprung (destroying drive alignment).
11—Foreign matter wedged in teeth.
12—Lack of lubrication.
13—Eccentric gear.
14—Shaft bearings or bushings worn.
15—Roughened camshaft thrust plunger tapping against gear housing cover.
16—Gears etched by acid formed in lubricating oil.

Fuel Knock

1—Compression knock due to carbon in cylinders.
2—Wrong kind of fuel used. Anti-knock fuel is recommended.

Oil Pump Noise

1—Pump plunger loose (plunger-type pump).
2—Pump plunger soft (plunger-type pump).
3—Cam operating plunger rough (plunger-type pump).
4—Pump shaft out of alignment.
5—Oil pressure too high.
6—Oil discharge line obstructed.
7—Vibration of oil pipes.
8—Worn pump housing or gears.
9—Pump thrust bearing or washer worn.
10—Pump drive gears worn.
11—Crankshaft bearing oil groove of such nature as to abruptly shut off flow of oil to bearings.
12—Loud buzz or vibration transmitted from relief valve to gauge. Cover oil line with rubber tubing to muffle noise.
13—No provision for release of pressure generated at point of contact of gear teeth.
14—Pressure fluctuation due to opening and closing of relief valve. Valve too small or spring too weak.

Popping in Carburetor

1—*See* Carburetor Trouble Analysis.

Spark Knock at High Speed with Loss of Speed

1—Ignition not properly timed (set too far advanced for high compression engine; re-time the ignition to maker's specifications).
2—Automatic spark advance not functioning at high speed.
3—Too much carbon in cylinders.
4—Carburetor set too lean.
5—Weak spring tension in automatic advance mechanism altering spark advance.

Jingling Noise

1—Loose oil deflector between crankshaft and its gear.
2—Broken inner valve spring.

Whistle or Shriek Occurring with Partially Open Throttle

1—Caused by sharp edge in path of incoming mixture of fuel and air vapor. On some installations, this is due to the heat riser tube becoming loose and dropping down to expose a sharp edge to the mixture passing through the riser.

Popping in Muffler

1—Gasoline mixture is too rich.
2—Engine misfiring badly due to ignition trouble.
3—Gasoline mixture too lean.
4—Spark or valve timing set late.
5—Exhaust valves not seating due to weak springs.
6—Lack of push rod clearance, warped, or corroded valves.

Exhaust Hissing

1—Spark plug leaking due to a defective gasket.
2—Exhaust manifold gasket broken.
3—Exhaust pipe loose in manifold.
4—Exhaust manifold retaining nuts loose.
5—Sand hole in exhaust manifold.
6—Defective cylinder-head gasket.
7—Priming cup leaking.

Rumbling Noise from Open Exhaust

1—Mixture too rich.
2—Choke valve stuck partly closed or running with the choke closed.
3—Air inlet to carburetor obstructed (air cleaner clogged).
4—Auxiliary needle valve spring too strong (air valve carburetor).
5—Auxiliary needle valve does not seat with choke wide open.

Noisy Exhaust

1—Idling speed too low (requiring slow burning rich mixture).

2—Carbon in one or more ports in the exhaust manifold.

3—Gasket obstruction at one or more exhaust ports.

Hissing Sound in the Crankcase

1—Cylinder walls scored. Loose pistons or stuck rings permit "blow-by" and will be accompanied by a loss of power. Also indicated by smoke coming through breather and crankcase ventilating system.

Miscellaneous Knocks, Noises, and Rattles

1—Loose manifold heat control valve.

2—Loose spark plugs.

3—Piston pin knock due to oil draining from cylinder wall. Will disappear as engine reaches normal operating temperature.

4—Generator armature does not rotate freely.

5—Starter armature laminations damaged. Problems 4 and 5 are due to worn bearings, bent shaft, bearings binding on shaft, excessive end play, and loose pole shoes.

6—Engine overheating. *See* Engine Overheats.

7—Poor grade of fuel. Not suited to engine.

8—Generator brushes squeaking. Too much spring tension on brushes, loose brush holder, brush not seating properly or of wrong type.

9—Water pump impeller broken. Pin or key sheared.

10—Muffler shell loose.

11—Exhaust pipe loose.

12—Exhaust pipe gasket blown.

13—Dust pans loose.

14—*See also* Clutch, Transmission, Universal Joints, Rear Axle, Body. Noise might not originate in the engine, but it might appear to come from that source.

Distributor Knock

1—Misalignment of the distributor drive.

2—Excessive end play in camshaft.

Squeaks

1—Generator brushes too hard.

2—Dry generator bearings.

3—Sticking valve or bent valve stem.

4—Dry valve tappet, push rod, or lifter.

5—Dry fan bearings.

6—Dry water pump bearings.

7—Loose fan blades.

Sharp Snap Heard Frequently when on Pull

1—High-tension wire insulation damaged.

2—Distributor head cracked.

3—High-tension wire loose in socket at distributor.

4—Spark plug gaps too wide.

5—Spark plug insulator cracked.

6—*See also* Electrical System for conditions causing noise in electrical units.

ENGINE LUBRICATION

Engine lubrication troubles become evident through high oil consumption. There are additional conditions that result from inefficient or overlubrication. These factors are included in the following analysis.

Oil Pumping

1—Main and connecting rod bearing clearance excessive or too much end clearance at connecting rod bearings.

2—Connecting rod bearings have excessive clearance at sides of bearing permitting escape of too much oil.

3—Excessive oil pressure. Too much oil in the oil pan or a defective pressure relief valve.

4—Oil diluted or too thin.

5—Ventilator or breather clogged.

6—Loose piston pins when pressure is lubricated.

7—Worn piston rings.

8—Piston ring gaps too small.

9—Piston rings fitted to cause uneven cylinder wall pressure.

10—Poor ring seat in piston groove.

11—Piston rings loose in piston grooves.

12—Distortion of ring under heat and normal wear.

13—Bent connecting rod.

14—Too much clearance behind compression rings.

15—Cylinders and pistons worn out-of-round and tapered.

16—Distorted pistons.

17—Too little clearance behind oil-regulating or oil-control rings.

18—Oil-regulating and oil-control ring groove bleed holes clogged.

19—Inner rings fouled with carbon.

Excessive Oil Consumption

1—Partially obstructed breather or ventilating system.

2—Bent connecting rods.

3—Use of the wrong kind of oil.

4—Excessive oil pressure.

5—Leaky intake valve guides.

6—Too much oil reaching valve chambers.

7—Mechanical condition of engine. *See* Oil Pumping.

8—Oil leakage. *See* Oil Leakage.

9—Improper bearing oil groove. Too much oil reaching connecting rod bearings.

10—Improper fitting of bearing shell in its seat allowing oil to escape before reaching bearing surface.

11—Scored thrust faces on crankshaft cheeks or side faces of connecting rods damaged.

12—Connecting rod and cap not properly aligned.

13—Broken vacuum pump diaphragm in combination fuel and vacuum pump.

Excessive Oil Dilution

1—Character of fuel used.

2—Excessive use of choke when manually operated.

3—Sticking choke when automatically controlled.

4—Unnecessary idling of engine.

5—Poor or erratic ignition.

6—Faulty carburetor adjustment or flooding of carburetor.

7—Wrong kind of oil used.

8—Mechanical condition of engine. *See* Oil Pumping.

Oil Leakage

1—Poorly fitted or worn front and rear main bearings.

2—Defective welch plug in rear camshaft bearing.

3—Clogged drain in rear main or camshaft bearing.

4—Defective gaskets at front end and defective wicks in rear main bearing cap.

5—Loose oil deflector in front end of engine.

6—Improper ventilation of crankcase.

7—Excessive "blow-by" at pistons.

8—Oil pressure too high.

9—Oil excessively diluted or too thin.

10—Leaks in external connections of system.

11—Oil pan cap screws not drawn tight.

12—Damaged oil pan gaskets or end packings.

13—Excessive end play in crankshaft.

14—Valve cover not tight or damaged.

15—Clutch and flywheel unit revolving at high speed (functioning as a blower). This creates a partial vacuum at the center of the shaft to assist oil in finding its way through the rear main bearing. See that clutch housing is properly ventilated.

Rapid Accumulation of Carbon in Cylinders

1—Thin, diluted, or the wrong kind of oil used.

2—Bearings in poor condition permitting excessive oil consumption.

3—Rich fuel mixture.

4—Driving with carburetor choked; automatic choke control sticking.
5—Low-grade fuel used.
6—Late ignition.

Oil Gauge Reading Fluctuates

1—Oil supply in the crankcase low.
2—Defective oil gauge.
3—Pump shaft and housing are worn. This permits the pump to suck air.

Low Oil Pressure

1—Thin, diluted or the wrong grade of oil used.
2—Bearings in poor condition. Excessive leakage prevents pressure from reaching the proper value.
3—Clearance between oil pump gear face and the cover is too large or the gasket is too thick.
4—Leaks in tubing and connections between pump and bearings. Also between oil pump and oil filter or oil gauge.
5—Defective pressure-relief valve.
6—Defective oil gauge.
7—Slow leak in pump suction line.
8—Bearing shells not properly seated in the crankcase or connecting rods.
9—At high-speed, insufficient oil reaching pump due to clogged screen.
10—Oil filter cartridge loose (shutting off oil flow).

No Oil Pressure Indicated, Engine Running

1—Oil supply exhausted.
2—Ice in crankcase oil pan.
3—Thick oil.
4—Defective oil gauge.
5—Screen at pump clogged.
6—Broken tube or connection in system.
7—Clogged oil tube leading to gauge.
8—Oil tube to gauge air bound.
9—*See also* Electric and Pressure-Type Oil Gauge.

High Oil Pressure Indicated

1—Defective oil gauge.
2—Oil pressure relief valve inoperative.
3—Incorrect adjustment of pressure relief valve.
4—Lack of necessary end clearance at connecting rod bearings.
5—Oil return from pressure relief valve clogged.
6—At low speed with engine warm, clogged oil line.

Sludge Forms in Oil Pan

1—Water in oil. *See* accumulation of water and ice.

Water or Ice Accumulates in Oil Pan

1—Car used mostly on short runs.
2—Failure to replace oil at frequent intervals.
3—Radiator not covered in extremely cold weather.
4—Defective cylinder head gasket, cracked cylinder wall, head or valve seat.
5—Excessive "blow-by" due to mechanical condition of engine. Water vapor is a product of combustion and in this case condenses in the crankcase to dilute the oil.
6—Unsuitable oil used.

Oil Freezes in Oil Pan

1—*See* above on sludge, water and ice.

Insufficient Oiling of Pistons and Cylinders

1—Oil supply low in crankcase.
2—Low oil pressure.
3—Insufficient clearance at sides of connecting rod bearings or clogged metering hole in bearings.
4—Oil metering hole not properly positioned due to improper assembly of connecting rod.

High Oil Temperature

1—When provision is made for controlling oil temperature due to oil regulator being clogged.

Oil Pump Loses Prime

1—Oil diluted or viscosity too low.
2—Defective relief valve or pump. Gears and housing worn excessively.
3—Poor gaskets permitting air leaks.

ENGINE TEST WITH VACUUM GAUGE

Needle Drops Back at Regular Intervals

1—Valves stuck open.
2—Chipped valve head.
3—Warped valve seat.
4—Tight valves.

Needle Drops Back at Irregular Intervals

1—Gummy valve stems.
2—Mixture too rich.
3—Mixture too lean.
4—Occasional plug miss.

Gauge Reading Low and Steady

1—Late valve timing.
2—Poor piston rings or oil.

Needle Floats Slowly Through Small Angle

1—Spark plug gaps too small.
2—Breaker points not synchronized.
3—Carburetor out of alignment.

Needle Flickers Getting Worse with Speed

1—Weak valve springs.
2—Loose valve guides.

Very Heavy Irregular Drop

1—Leaky cylinder head gasket.
2—Obstructed exhaust. Choked muffler.

Low Vacuum

1—Intake manifold leak.

Note: Vacuum gauge readings should be taken at idling speed. The average engine will draw from 16 to 18 inches vacuum at the proper idling speed. Commercial vehicle engines will draw from 16 to 20 inches vacuum under similar conditions. When the engine is properly tuned and in proper mechanical condition, the gauge needle will always be steady. If not, something is wrong with the engine.

ENGINE OVERHEATS

Imperfect Operation of Cooling System

1—Insufficient water in system.
2—Excessive quantity of antifreeze in system.
3—Cooling medium frozen.
4—Obstruction in path of water from block to head.
5—Defective or wrong type of cylinder-head gasket.
6—Transfer holes in cylinder-head gasket too small obstructing circulation.
7—Defective thermostat (not opening at proper temperature).
8—Engine water jackets coated with scale.
9—Sand not completely removed from system.
10—Too much of radiator surface covered.
11—Replacement core capacity is too small.
12—Radiator water passages clogged with dirt or lime.
13—Radiator water passages pinched or dented.
14—Radiator air cells or passages insulated with dirt or paint, or reduced due to radiator being frozen.

15—Radiator baffle plate loose (obstructing flow of water through core).

16—Radiator shutter pivots and linkage frozen so that thermostats or manual control cannot function.

17—Thermostat not properly connected to shutters.

18—Radiator surface obstructed by accessories.

19—Radiator overflow clogged, pinched, or blocked by filler cap affecting proper venting of system.

20—Air pockets in cooling system.

21—Radiator hose collapsed or blocked (careless installation).

22—Defective water pump. *See* Pump Inoperative.

23—Fan belt too loose or blades too flat.

24—Oil on fan belt or excessive friction of fan due to lack of lubrication.

25—Fan drive pulley key sheared.

26—Obstruction to free flow of air under hood.

27—Water distributing tube clogged with rust or corrosion (especially on cars with high mileage).

28—Bypass-type thermostat removed and coolant not circulating through radiator. Bypass must be closed to operate engine without thermostat.

Thermostat Fails (Inoperative)

1—Hose clamp too tight (causing valve to stick). Applies only to type mounted in outlet hose.

2—Thermostat installed upside down.

3—Dirt or pieces of rubber hose imbedded on the edge of the butterfly valve holding the valve open or closed.

4—Failure to expel all air from cooling system when filling the radiator. Run the engine a few minutes and then add water.

5—With low-boiling-point antifreeze, watch the liquid level in the radiator and replace evaporated solution.

Note: Do not be misled by a defective heat indicator. Be sure this instrument is not defective when its reading is the source of complaint.

Imperfect Operation of Lubrication System

1—Insufficient oil in oil pan.

2—Improper grade or poor quality of oil.

3—Oil excessively diluted or too thin.

4—Insufficient oil pressure.

5—Oil pump not functioning.

6—Excessive friction in engine due to tight bearings and pistons.

7—Overlubrication causing excessive carbon.

8—Oil too heavy for system.

9—High oil temperature due to clogged oil temperature regulator or cooler.

Note: In connection with this subject, also refer to the trouble analysis of the engine lubrication system.

Ignition Defects Causing Overheating

1—Ignition not properly timed.
2—Driving with spark too far retarded.
3—Automatic spark advance inoperative or operating too freely.
4—Pitted breaker points.
5—Breaker spring too weak.
6—Dual breakers not synchronized.
7—Defective spark plugs. *See* Spark Plugs.
8—Defective condenser.
9—Defective high-tension cables reducing spark intensity.
10—Excessive play in distributor drive affecting spark timing.
11—Short circuit in distributor.

Note: The last two items also cause misfiring. *See* also Ignition System.

Mechanical Defects in Engine Causing Overheating

1—Engine stiff due to tight bearings and pistons.
2—Ineffective lubrication.
3—Excessive carbon in cylinders.
4—Piston and rings improperly fitted. Too much wall tension or high friction.
5—Scored cylinder walls.
6—Worn timing chain or gears affecting valve timing.
7—Valves not properly timed.
8—Valves not seating properly.
9—Broken or weak valve springs.
10—Compression too high for fuel used.
11—Engine forced to operate for long periods in low gear.

Carburetion Defects Causing Overheating

1—Improper carburetor adjustment.
2—Wrong jets in carburetor.
3—Carburetor automatic controls not functioning.
4—Too much heat applied to mixture.
5—Heat riser tube burned through.
6—Heat valve not operating in exhaust manifold.
7—Bakelite insulator between carburetor and manifold burned out.
8—Fuel boiling in system (vapor lock).
9—*See also* Carburetor and Fuel System.

Exhaust System Defects Causing Overheating

1—Manifold heat control valve improperly installed.
2—Manifold heat control valve stuck closed.
3—Muffler clogged.
4—Muffler tail pipe clogged or dented.

Chassis Defects Causing Overheating

1—Tires not properly inflated.
2—Wheels out of alignment.
3—Brakes dragging.
4—Clutch slipping.
5—Tight wheel bearings.
6—Tight transmission or pinion shaft bearings.
7—Tight differential bearings.
8—Cracked or broken transmission, axle, or wheel bearing.
9—Rear axle shafts or propeller shaft binding.
10—Dry universal joints; propeller shaft bent or out of balance.
11—Rear axle out of alignment.
12—Excessive chassis friction due to lack of lubrication.
13—Too much oil in transmission or differential unit.

Water Pump Impeller

1—Pump impeller loose (pin or key sheared).
2—Pump shaft broken.
3—Excessive wear between sides of impeller and pump housing.
4—Pump drive coupling broken.
5—Defective fan belt when driven by fan.
6—Defective packing permits pump to suck air.

Radiator Leaks

1—Radiator frozen.
2—Radiator tie (rod loose).
3—Radiator cushion pad hardened.
4—Radiator hold-down bolts loose.
5—Back pressure (clogged overflow vent).

Thermostat Inoperative

1—Clamp around the thermostat too tight (causing butterfly valve to stick).
2—Thermostat installed upside down.
3—Dirt or pieces of rubber hose imbedded on edge of butterfly valve (holding valve either open or closed).
4—Failure to expel air from the cooling system when filling radiator.
5—Low liquid level in the radiator (especially with low-boiling point antifreeze solutions).
6—Bellows-type punctured bellows.
7—Bellows-type relief hole clogged permitting steam pressure to lock thermostat.

Foaming with Antifreeze in System

1—Air being drawn into cooling system through loose pump packings.

Leakage Requiring Frequent Refilling

1—Defective pump packings.
2—Defective pump gaskets.
3—Pump shaft worn or scored.
4—Pump out of alignment.
5—Leaky hose connections.
6—Defective cylinder-head gasket.
7—Defective gaskets in the cooling system.
8—Radiator leaking.
9—Engine overheating (loss of water through overflow).
10—Defective baffle plates in the radiator (water siphoning through overflow vent; baffle plate closing passage through core).
11—Evaporation due to boiling when the engine continually overheats.
12—Partly clogged radiator core (pump forcing water through overflow).

Engine Slops Water and then Overheats

1—Radiator core clogged; pump forcing water through overflow to reduce volume and permit overheating.
2—Bypass-type thermostat removed and not replaced or bypass closed to permit normal circulation.

Loss of Water by Boiling

1—Due to hard driving, high speed, and quick stops (causing surge of coolant).
2—Defective thermostat.

Boiling or Slopping when Engine Is Stopped

1—Steam pockets in water jackets of cylinder block.
2—Bypass-type thermostat removed, pump forcing water out of overflow with radiator core clogged.
3—Air suction through pump causing foaming and loss of water through overflow.

System cannot be Filled Completely

1—Airbound due to plugged thermostat. Fill system and run the engine to heat the water. This will open the thermostat to permit complete filling.

Water on Top of Cylinders

1—Cylinder-head joints leak.
2—Cylinder head cracked.
3—Defective cylinder-head gasket.
4—Cylinder-head studs or bolts loose.
5—Upper hose connection leaks.
6—Sand hole in casting permitting seepage.

Grease or Oil in Water

1—Wrong type of grease used at pump.
2—Leaky cylinder-head gasket.
3—Cracked cylinder wall or cylinder head.
4—Cracked valve seat.

Engine Overheats, Slows Down, Stops, or Misfires when Throttle Is Closed Suddenly

1—This condition is caused by what is known as *vapor lock*. Bubbles form in the fuel line and the carburetor float chamber due to boiling fuel in the system. Condition is aggravated by applying too much heat to the fuel. *See* Analysis of Carburetor Troubles.

BATTERY IGNITION SYSTEM

Engine Will Not Start

1—Breaker arm rubbing block broken.
2—Breaker arm spring weak or broken.
3—Breaker points burned or dirty.
4—Distributor cap cracked or broken.
5—Grounded rotor due to crack in rotor.
6—Rotor spring broken.
7—Condenser shorted or open.
8—Defective insulation on primary wires, poor connection, or broken wire.
9—Defective coil. An open circuit in secondary winding will cause coil to fail when spark is under compression even though coil tests OK on test stand.
10—Coil burned out or damp.
11—Resistance unit on coil defective.
12—Loose connections in ignition circuit.
13—Ignition switch defective.
14—Battery weak or fully discharged.
15—*See also* Engine will not Start (under subheading Engine).

Engine fails to start when cranked by starting motor with ignition switch "on." Charge indicator or ammeter flickers to discharge while engine is cranked.

1—Breaker points fail to open properly (readjust gap).
2—Badly pitted points. Note if an extra condenser has been connected to distributor terminal to eliminate radio interference. Remove condenser and connect to positive side of coil. Redress points.
3—Defective condenser.
4—Broken down ignition coil (replace).
5—Poor high tension cable insulation.
6—Incorrect ignition timing.

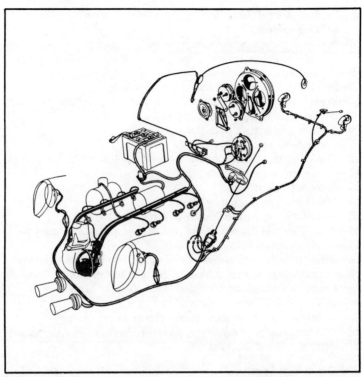

Ignition system.

7—Charge indicator or ammeter does not flicker. Open primary circuit in coil. Replace coil.

Engine Lacks Power; Sluggish Acceleration

1—Ignition not properly timed (set late).
2—Automatic spark advance not functioning properly.
3—Weak or damp ignition coil.
4—Breaker points not properly adjusted; poor contact or weak breaker arm spring.
5—Breaker points not properly synchronized when dual breaker points are used.
6—Wear of distributor mechanism disturbing synchronism of breakers.
7—Defective or wrong type of spark plugs.

Engine Misfires

1—Breaker grounded causing weak spark at plug.
2—Metal chips or dirt on breaker base. Primary current does not drop to zero.

3—Breaker worn or loose (evident by misfiring in certain positions of advance or retard).

4—Breaker arm rubbing block worn (causing small contact point opening. Contacts might be burned. Excessive breaker arm spring tension.

5—Breaker point gap too wide; misfiring at high speed.

6—Breaker gap too narrow; misfiring at low speed.

7—Breaker points burned (damaged condenser or high voltage in circuit).

8—Breaker arm spring weak or broken.

9—Breaker arm contact plate screw loose.

10—Condenser open (weak spark).

11—Condenser shorted (excessive arcing at points).

12—Grounded rotor due to crack in rotor.

13—Rotor spring broken.

14—Distributor cap cracked or broken.

15—Distributor cap burned (engine misfires regularly).

16—Bent or burned distributor cap contacts (misfiring on a heavy pull).

17—Poorly grounded distributor or coil.

18—Improper high-tension wiring (misfiring in one or more cylinders).

19—Defective high-tension cables (misfiring in one or more cylinders).

20—Defective low-tension wire; poor connections or broken wires.

21—Current leakage at secondary cables.

22—Vacuumatic spark advance causing change in breaker gap.

23—Broken pig tail wire inside insulation in connection between coil wire terminal and contact point arm.

Misfiring at High Speed

1—Gum and corrosion on steel balls, serving as a bearing for spark advance plate, forms a poor ground.

Engine Hesitates at High Speed

1—Vacuum advance sticking to retard normal centrifugal advance of spark.

Engine Lopes at Low Speed

1—Can be due to distributor cap not being properly seated.

2—Ignition not timed properly.

3—Vacuum spark control not functioning to retard spark due to leakage in vacuum line or chamber.

Engine Cuts Out at High Speed

1—Erratic ignition due to loose or weak breaker.

2—Worn distributor cam or fiber rubbing block.

3—Excessive wear in distributor drive and mounting.

4—Poor distributor ground.

5—Wrong type coil used.

6—Soft or worn distributor carbon brush.

Poor Acceleration

1—Spark plug gaps too wide.
2—Ignition timed late.
3—Faulty ignition causing engine to hesitate when accelerating.
4—*See also* Misfiring and Sluggish Acceleration.

Engine Hesitates when Accelerating

1—Faulty ignition causing misfiring when accelerating.
2—*See also* reasons for faulty ignition listed above. High-tension wires from distributor to coil should be separated from other high-tension wires to avoid current leakage.
3—On a fast start, break in distributor flexible lead at breaker plate (primary terminal to contact arm).

Engine Knock on Pull or when Accelerating

1—Ignition timed too early.
2—Automatic spark advance stuck.
3—Vacuum spark control does not control spark.

Engine Fires Regularly with Switch "Off"

1—Defective switch; does not break circuit.
2—Short circuit between motor and generator field windings.
3—Spark plugs overheated (running too hot).

Preignition

1—Caused by very high combustion chamber temperatures.
2—Mixture too lean.
3—Leaks in intake manifold or carburetor flanges.
4—Spark plugs not securely tightened in cylinder head.
5—Excessive carbon in cylinders.
6—*See also* Spark Plugs.

Engine Overheats

1—Ignition timed late.

No Spark or Weak Spark at Plugs

1—Defective ignition coil. Shorted primary or open secondary winding. Grounded primary terminal due to defective insulation.
2—Defective rotor or distributor head.
3—Dirty track in distributor head.
4—Worn distributor shaft bearings.
5—Defective high-tension wiring.
6—Defective condenser.

7—Breaker points dirty or pitted due to defective condenser or high voltage in circuit.

8—Breaker points not properly adjusted.

9—Shorted resistance unit on coil.

10—Dirty or cracked spark plug insulator.

11—Spark plugs not properly adjusted.

12—Loose connections or open circuit at ignition switch or relay.

13—Battery weak or discharged.

14—Distributor with vacuum control. Poor ground between breaker plate and subplate due to leak in ground lead.

15—Distributor with vacuum control; break in lead between primary terminal and breaker arm.

Track in Distributor Requires Frequent Cleaning

1—Rough cam surface or rotor button.

2—Track roughened by use of sandpaper for cleaning.

3—Breaker arm set too high causing rotor button to bottom in rotor.

Coil Weak

1—Coil leaks wax due to overheating; primary shorted or loose connections between generator and battery.

2—Ignition current abnormally large (shorted primary winding).

Breaker Points Arc and Burn Excessively

1—Oil on distributor parts. Wear of rubbing block.

2—Resistance unit out of circuit.

3—Defective condenser.

4—Breaker points not properly adjusted (gap too small).

5—Spark plug gaps too wide.

6—High voltage due to open circuit, dirty, or loose commutator on generator.

7—Bouncing of points possible due to too long a cam angle.

8—Bouncing of points due to worn distributor shaft bearing.

9—Weak breaker arm spring.

10—On rubber-mounted engine, battery ground strap changed from power plant to frame causing high resistance.

11—High primary amperage.

12—High primary voltage.

13—Full generator potential imposed on primary by poor ground at battery or ammeter.

Defective Vacuum Spark Control

1—Partially clogged passages in carburetor.

2—Vacuum leak at unit.

3—Defective spring in unit.

4—Binding in distributor.

Vacuum Spark Advance Sluggish

1—Kink in vacuum tube.
2—*See also* Defective Vacuum Spark Control.

Ignition Current Does Not Drop to Zero when Points Separate

1—Primary winding grounded.
2—Damaged or defective insulation.
3—Shorted condenser.
4—Metal chips or dirt on distributor breaker plate.
5—Contact arm in switch touching case of coil.

Ignition Current Abnormally Large

1—Primary winding shorted.
2—Damaged or defective insulation in coil.
3—Overheating of coil.

No Spark from Coil; No Primary Current

1—Primary winding open-circuited.
2—Primary winding burned out.
3—Lead broken.
4—Switch points dirty or not making contact.

Weak Spark; Primary Current Normal

1—Secondary winding grounded.

High-Tension Cables Damaged

1—Engine misfires on one or more cylinders. Spark jumping from one cable to another.
2—Burned insulation contacting exhaust manifold.

Low-Tension Cable Damaged

1—Engine misfires or fails to start. Poor connections or defective insulation or broken wires.

IGNITION SWITCH

Engine Will Not Start

1—Defective switch.
2—Loose connections at switch.

Ignition Weak or Irregular

1—Poor contact at switch.
2—Switch spider weak or loose.
3—Contacts dirty or corroded.

BATTERY IGNITION DEFECTS NOTED ON TEST STAND

Spark Plug Current Low

1—Corroded terminals.
2—Defective high tension wiring.
3—Poor contact in distributor.

Current Low to Half the Number of Plugs

1—Breaker not adjusted with equal gap.
2—Breaker cam worn.
3—Too much play in distributor shaft.
4—With dual coils, one coil weak.

Irregular Current to Spark Plugs

1—Cracked distributor.
2—Poor rotor contact.
3—Low voltage in primary circuit.
4—Defective wiring.

Ignition Advanced Too Far

1—Indicated by fluctuation of vacuum gauge needle during vacuum test.

Irregular Current on High Speed Test

1—Poor connections in circuit.
2—Defective breaker points.
3—Breaker brush sticking on shaft.
4—Defective condenser.

MAGNETO IGNITION SYSTEM

Engine Will Not Start

1—Breaker points not making proper contact.
2—Breaker points gap too large.
3—Breaker level sticks.
4—Shorted primary circuit.
5—Switch closed (switch or switch wire shorted).
6—Short between coil and distributor brush.

Sudden Failure

1—Faulty connections at switch.
2—Disconnected switch wires.
3—Short circuited in low tension wires.
4—Defective distributor carbon brush.
5—Presence of dirt or moisture.

Engine Will Not Stop

1—Engine overheating causing preignition.

2—Broken ground wire.

3—Broken connection between magneto and coil.

4—Magneto brushes not making contact.

Engine Lacks Power

1—Magnets improperly assembled.

2—Magnets weak (need recharging).

Loss of Power

1—Magneto not timed properly.

2—Magnets weak.

Misfiring at Low Speed

1—Spark plug gaps too wide or too narrow.

2—Breaker gap too large.

3—Magneto dirty or poorly adjusted.

4—Carbon brushes making poor contact.

5—Loose connections.

6—Weak magnets.

Misfiring at High Speed

1—Breaker gap too small.

2—Breaker arm not operating freely.

3—Loose connections.

Misfiring at All Speeds

1—Defective or dirty spark plugs.

2—Improper spark gap.

3—Cable insulation chafed.

4—Cable connections loose.

5—Breaker contacts dirty.

6—Breaker lever sticks.

7—Breaker points out of adjustment.

8—Dirty distributor.

9—Brush holder cracked.

No Spark

1—Magneto not timed properly.

2—Dirty distributor (covered with oil or carbon).

3—Contacts do not break at proper time.

4—Contacts burned.

5—Rubbing block badly worn.

6—Weak breaker spring.

Weak Spark

1—Magnets reversed in assembly.

2—Breaker points carboned, pitted, or worn.

3—Defective distributor brush.
4—Brush on the collector ring cracked.
5—Weak magnets.

Magneto Dead

1—Oil in the breaker housing.
2—Breaker points carboned, pitted, or worn.
3—Breaker arm sticking.
4—Breaker points not properly adjusted.
5—Distributor brushes worn.
6—Distributor gear improperly set.
7—Breaker cam improperly set.
8—Defective condenser.
9—Wrong type of brush on the collector ring.
10—Defective carbon brushes.
11—Loose connections at breaker terminals.
12—Defective ground between switch and magneto.
13—Poor spring tension at the collector brush.
14—Sheared drive coupling.
15—Defective magneto armature.

Breaker Points Burned

1—Breaker points worn or pitted.
2—Breaker points not properly adjusted.
3—Defective condenser.
4—Weak breaker spring.

Squeaks

1—Armature shaft bearings dry.

Defective Collector Ring

1—Defective insulation in mounting.

Condenser

1—Short circuited.
2—Open circuited.

Defective Armature

1—Defective collector ring.
2—Open primary winding.
3—Open secondary winding.
4—Shorted primary or secondary.

Armature Out of Alignment

1—Worn bearings or broken ball in bearing.

2—Gears meshed too tight.

3—Loose screws on armature head.

Armature Rubs Pole Piece

1—Worn bearings.

2—Loose screws in armature head.

3—Gears meshed too tight.

SPARK PLUGS

Engine Loses Power

1—Wrong type plug used.

2—Insulator pale white after plug has been in use for some time. Shell has blue, brown or red tinge (showing overheating and preignition). Plug running too hot; change to cooler-running plug. Make sure fuel is suited to engine.

3—Insulator cracked on the lower end. Cooler-running plug might be required.

4—Upper part of insulator blackened just above shell (indicating "blow-by"). Plug much too hot; use cooler plug.

5—If plugs are of the right type, check breaker points, high-tension cables, seating or exhaust valves, and timing of engine.

Engine Hard to Start

1—Spark plug gaps too wide.

2—Spark plug gaps too narrow.

3—Insulator covered with black soot. Check carburetor adjustment and operation of choke. If habitual, change to hotter-running plug.

4—Plug wet or oily; insulator coated with carbon. Mixture might be too rich or oil pumping is taking place.

5—Insulator broken on upper end. This can be due to abuse in removing or replacing the plug.

6—Plug gap filled with oil but not carboned. Check for various causes of hard starting and also oil pumping.

7—Plugs in good condition (proper type), but engine misfires. Plugs might be worn out. Check ignition system and cables.

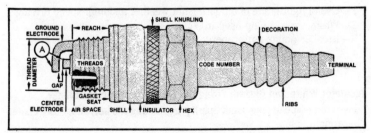

Spark plug.

Spark Plugs Require Frequent Cleaning

1—Oil pumping. *See* Engine Lubrication.
2—Rich mixture. *See* Carburetor.
3—Insufficient heat at carburetor. Mixture wet. Automatic heat control stuck.
4—Low-grade fuel used.
5—Wrong Grade of oil used. Flash and fire test of oil too low.
6—Misfiring in cylinder at fault.

Fouling of Spark Plugs

1—Brownish or reddish coating on insulator indicates dust or dirt.
2—Wet, shiny-black coating indicates overoiling.
3—Sooty, dry-black coating indicates rich mixture (imperfect combustion).

Spark Plugs Badly Burned

1—Plug not properly tightened.
2—Improper wrench used when installing.
3—Plug running too hot.
4—Exhaust valve overheated causing preignition and abnormal temperature in combustion chamber.
5—Valve tappets have too little clearance.
6—Valves sticking in guides.
7—Improper valve seating.
8—Retarded spark.
9—Detonation and overheating of plug due to excessive spark advance.
10—Lean mixture.
11—Carbon in combustion chamber.
12—Inadequate cooling of plug due to insufficient water in or defect in cooling system.

Spark Plugs Foul

1—Due to rich mixture, dull black appearance of insulator.
2—Due to loss of compression, dull black appearance of insulator.
3—Due to oil fouling, shiny black appearance of insulator.

Spark Plugs Moist or Carboned

1—Use of light-grade of oil during hot weather and high-speed driving.
2—Wrong type of plug used (too cold).
3—Breaker points not properly adjusted.
4—Mixture too rich.
5—Engine pumping oil.

Insulator White and Glazed; Firing Tip Shows Tendency to Blister

1—Wrong type of plug used. Spark plug running too hot; substitute cooler running plug.

Blow-By at Plugs

Indicated by greyish-black streaks on the insulator top just above the shell.

1—Plugs operate at abnormally high temperatures.
2—Careless at abnormally high temperatures.
3—Use of improper wrench.
4—*See also* Plugs Badly Burned.

Oxide Deposits

1—Due to fuel used. Certain types of fuel will cause a rusty-brown oxide coating on the insulator.

Broken Insulator Top

1—Careless handling.
2—Improper installation.
3—Wrench striking plug.
4—Loose fitting wrench.

Insulator Split at Lower End

1—Bending or straining of center electrode (adjust side electrode only to set gap).

Side Electrode Excessively Worn

1—Plug not properly tightened.
2—Plug running too hot.
3—Use of high output coil (especially when lower tip of insulator shows no signs of excessive heat).

Misfiring at All Speeds

1—Fouled spark plugs.
2—Porcelain insulator cracked.
3—Plug gaps too wide or too narrow. Plugs that fire are warm; plugs that do not fire are cold.

Misfiring at High Speed

1—Spark plug gaps too wide.

Misfiring at Low Speed or Idling

1—Spark plug gaps too narrow.

Misfiring at Low Speed on Pull

1—Spark plug gaps too wide.

CARBURETOR

In analyzing carburetor trouble, it is necessary to give due consideration to the behavior of the engine. Difficulties arising due to the mechanical condition of the engine and its various accessories that affect performance must also be kept in mind.

Excessive Fuel Consumption (Low Gasoline Mileage)

1—Habits of driver involving improper use of manually operated choke and heat controls. Excessive idling of engine, short runs with sufficient stops to allow engine to cool. Pumping accelerator pedal.

2—Imperfect fuel mixture. Choke might not open fully. Auxiliary needle valve, when employed, might not seat with choke wide open. Carburetor not properly adjusted or flooding.

3—Carburetor, vacuum tank, or fuel pump and fuel lines too hot; too much heated air. Insulate carburetor and fuel system. Check heat control and shield air intake.

4—Fuel lost due to leakage. *See* Flooding and Dripping at Carburetor when Engine is Stopped.

5—Bypass needle valve stuck open.

6—Engine needs a tune-up.

7—Improper spark timing or inoperative automatic spark control.

8—Poor compression due to mechanical condition of engine, tappets adjusted too close, or valves do not seat.

9—Engine misfiring. *See* Engine Misfires.

10—Overheating of engine. *See* Engine Overheats.

11—Fuel syphoning through accelerating pump discharge jet.

12—Excessive friction in engine. Pistons, connecting rod, and main bearings too tight.

13—Dragging brakes. Tight wheel bearings. Lack of proper lubrication of transmission, universal joints, and rear axle creating high rolling resistance.

14—Tires underinflated.

15—Economizer piston sticking holding power orifice at all times.

16—Idling speed too low requires excessively rich mixture.

17—Air leaks in vacuum operated accessories diluting mixture.

18—Excessively dirty air cleaner partially obstructing air inlet to carburetor.

19—High fuel pump pressure.

20—Air leak at float chamber cover gasket.

21—Improperly installed air cleaner.

22—Carburetor jets too large.

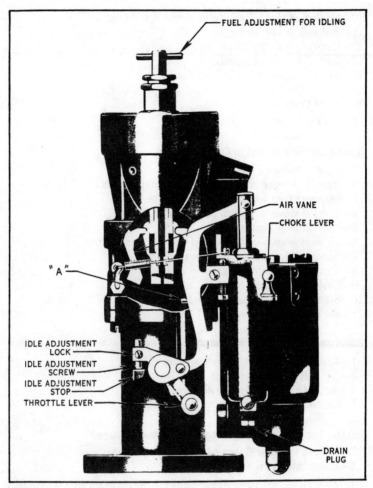

Carburetor.

Engine Will Not Idle

1—Fuel pump pressure too high at idle speed causes a loading condition.
2—Fuel level too high causes a loading condition at idling speed.
3—Air leaks at carburetor and manifold.
4—Poor or dirty fuel being used.
5—Jets and fuel passages or fuel pipes clogged.
6—Damaged compensator jet.
7—Attempting to idle engine at a speed too low for good idling.
8—Worn jets altering calibration of carburetor.
9—Needle valve and seat worn.

10—No flow of fuel to carburetor at idle speed range.
11—Bad seat at low speed jet.
12—Damaged idle adjustment screw.
13—Carbon in bore of carburetor.
14—Throttle valve not properly adjusted.

No Fuel at Carburetor

1—*See* Fuel System.

Insufficient Flow of Fuel to Carburetor

1—Float rubbing on float bowl.
2—Bent float lever or lever shaft preventing free action of float.
3—Incorrect float level.
4—Shut-off valve in system partly closed.
5—Fuel strainer clogged.
6—Strainer at carburetor clogged with ice or sediment.
7—Sharp bend or dirt in fuel pipes.
8—Vacuum tank vent clogged.
9—Leaks in fuel lines.
10—Standpipe in main tank above fuel level.
11—*See also* Fuel System.

Excessive Use of Choke Necessary

1—Caused by lean mixture adjustment.
2—Air leaks in intake system.
3—Air leaks in vacuum-operated accessories.
4—Carburetor flange mounting bolts loose.

Mixture Too Lean after Adjustment with Vacuum Gauge

1—Leak-in windshield wiper line must be corrected.
2—Leaky carburetor flange gasket.

NOTE: Air leaks will make it practically impossible to secure a satisfactory carburetor adjustment. Check all manifold joints and connections leading to devices operated by vacuum. Disconnect vacuum fittings at manifold and substitute pipe plugs to check for air leaks in manifold or carburetor. If no leaks exist, then leak must exist in fittings of one or more of the accessories operated by vacuum.

Irregular Idling

1—Carburetor too hot. Insulate carburetor and fuel lines to avoid boiling of fuel which causes a lean mixture or uneven flow of fuel.
2—Use of high-test fuel in hot weather.
3—Temperatures under the hood too high.
4—Air leaks in carburetor or manifold joints.

5—Dual carburetor throttles not synchronized.

6—Idle mixture passage clogged.

7—Leaks at main nozzle.

8—Heat riser burnt through diluting mixture with exhaust gas.

9—*See also* Engine Misfires.

Engine Stops when Throttle Is
Closed Suddenly or Misfiring at Regular Intervals

1—Vapor lock at idling tube or jet or use of high test fuel in hot weather. Too much heated air. Check heat control. Shield air intake if necessary. Place fuel line outside of frame.

2—Temperature under the hood too high.

3—Dual carburetors not properly synchronized.

Engine Stalls During Warm-Up

1—Choke held nearly closed.

Frosting of Carburetor

1—Air intake temperature too low.

2—Heat path to carburetor obstructed.

3—Heat control not properly adjusted.

4—Defective thermostat in heat control.

5—Heat riser shifted (cuts off flow of heat).

6—Improper mixture ratio.

7—No hot spot or effective heat valve.

Carburetor Floods

1—High fuel level.

2—Dirt on float needle or seat.

3—Imperfect valve or seat.

4—Wrong type valve or seat used.

5—Float rubbing on carburetor bowl.

6—Improper float level adjustment.

7—Bent float lever or lever shaft.

8—Choke valve improperly operated.

9—Carburetor float too heavy.

10—Broken gaskets in carburetor.

11—Sand hole in bowl casting.

12—Vacuum tank flooding.

13—Carburetor bowl retaining nut loose.

14—Air bleeder valve plugged (not permitting proper venting of main jet).

15—Excessive fuel line pressure caused by excessive vapor formation in fuel line.

16—Float valve and seat leaking because of being cocked or worn.

17—Float valve and seat do not match properly.

18—High fuel pump pressure.

19—*See also* Fuel Pump.

Carburetor Floods after Stopping Engine

1—Probably due to percolation. Substitute new carburetor with anti-percolating device.

Needle Valve Sticking

1—Due to gum forming in fuel caused by tank soldering flux and especially active on certain materials. A quart of alcohol added to a tank of fuel will usually dissolve the gum.

2—*See also* Gum Forms in Fuel.

High Fuel Level

1—Fuel pump pressure too high. The average carburetor will stand about 3 to 4 pounds maximum pressure.

2—Dirt under float valve.

3—Carburetor float logged (too heavy).

4—Incorrect float level adjustment.

5—Bent float lever or lever shaft.

6—Worn float valve.

7—When idling, float valve held open by dirt.

Dripping at Carburetor when Engine is Stopped

1—Condensation of fuel in manifold. This particularly happens in cold weather and must be expected.

2—Leaks in fuel pipes or fittings.

3—Leaky float chamber.

4—Fuel level in float chamber above fuel jet.

5—*See also* Carburetor Floods.

Carburetor Drains after Long Period of Idleness

1—Caused by capillary attraction due to condition of surface of metal in contact with fuel.

2—Defective casting permitting slow seepage.

Engine Cuts Out on Turn

1—Float logged. Partly filled with fuel causing flooding on turn.

Carburetor Floods on Rough Roads

1—Due to float shake resulting from vibration.

Loading

1—Float level too high.

2—Choke not fully open.

3—*See also* Automatic Choke Control.

Flooded Engine Will Not Unload

1—Improper adjustment of choke.

Improper Operation of Choke Control

1—Leak between manifold and control unit. Loose mounting bolts or defective gasket.

2—Improper adjustment between control and choke valve.

3—Sticking or binding in moving parts.

Back Firing or Popping in Carburetor

1—Cold engine.

2—Low-grade gasoline used.

3—Water in gasoline. During acceleration this can be detected by sputtering and popping in carburetor.

4—Lean fuel mixture or insufficient flow of fuel to the carburetor. Also can be due to partly clogged jets and fuel passages.

5—Weak spring on air valve carburetor.

6—Carburetor float sticking.

7—Vacuum tank or fuel pump defective. *See* Fuel System.

8—Worn throttle valve stem or shaft.

9—Air leaks in intake system.

10—Improper ignition timing or inoperative automatic spark control.

11—One or more intake valve lifters or valve stems stuck in guides. Lack of push rod clearance.

12—Improper valve timing.

13—Weak intake valve springs.

14—Carbon on valve seats. Warped valves.

15—Worn intake valve stems or guides.

16—Intake valve spring broken.

17—Spark plug wires crossed.

18—Moisture in distributor.

Poor Acceleration

1—Accelerating pump not properly adjusted.

2—Dirt in carburetor, fuel strainer, or fuel pipes.

3—Stiff engine will show sluggish acceleration.

4—Engine slow to warm up. *See* Automatic Heat Control.

5—Heat damper valve sticking in bushings.

6—Flexible fuel line collapsing to lean mixture.

7—With the engine well warmed up, carbon accumulation in heat riser section of intake manifold.

Lean Mixture with Partly or Fully Open Throttle

1—Improper carburetor adjustment.
2—Weak air valve spring in air valve carburetor.
3—Insufficient flow of fuel to float chamber.
4—Carburetor nozzles and jets partly clogged.
5—High-speed jet too small.

Lean Mixture with Throttle Closed

1—Air leaks due to leaky gaskets at carburetor or manifold.
2—Warped carburetor or intake manifold flange.
3—Low-speed idling adjustment too lean.
4—Low-speed nozzle or jet partly clogged.
5—Sand hole in intake manifold.
6—Insufficient flow of fuel to carburetor.

Flat Spot on Acceleration

1—Accelerating pump discharge too heavy.
2—Jet worn or loose in its seat.
3—Jet enlarged (altering calibration).
4—Defective pump jet gasket.
5—Restricted or damaged screen at pump.
6—Pump piston leaks.
7—Pump piston worn or sticking.
8—Leaky accelerating pump check valve.
9—Discharge valve leaks on intake stroke of pump.
10—Clogged pump vent.
11—Pump linkage worn.
12—Improper pump linkage adjustment. Charge too heavy in hot weather; too light in cold weather.
13—Accompanied by "ping." Too much heat applied to mixture.
14—Anti-percolator valve opening too early.
15—Main jet too lean.

Surge or Flat Spot above Idle Range

1—Improper seal between anti-percolator cap and seat admitting air.

Mixture Too Rich at all Speeds

1—Dirty air cleaner.
2—Choke valve stuck in air horn.
3—Choke valve not operating properly; sticking or rubbing on inside of air horn.
4—Bowl cover with vent installed on a balanced carburetor.

Mixture Too Rich with Throttle Partly Closed (Idle)

1—Low-speed jet worn or too large.

2—Air bleed holes restricted.
3—Idle port damaged.
4—Idle needle damaged prevents proper adjustment.
5—Carbon in bore around throttle valve.
6—Throttle valve improperly installed.

Mixture Too Rich at High Speed

1—High fuel pump pressure.
2—High float level.
3—Defective float bowl cover.
4—Main jet loose in seating.
5—Damaged nozzle.
6—Vented cover on balanced carburetor.
7—Dirty air cleaner.
8—Improperly adjusted choke.

Lean Mixture with Throttle Closed (Idle)

1—Air bleed holes oversize.
2—Economizer hole restricted.
3—Restriction in passage to low-speed jet.
4—Port hole restricted or port opening too small.
5—Restriction at idle needle seat.
6—Air leak at flange gasket.
7—Idle needle burred.
8—Port plug loose (not seating in casting).

Lean Mixture on Acceleration

1—Weak plunger springs.
2—Worn or dried out plunger leather.
3—Damaged or cracked plunger leather.
4—Intake or discharge check not seated.
5—Intake or discharge check sticking or leaking.
6—Pump passage clogged.
7—Pump jets restricted.
8—Pump not properly adjusted.
9—Worn pump linkage.

Lean Mixture at High Speed

1—Low fuel pump pressure.
2—Insufficient fuel in carburetor bowl.
3—Restricted bowl vent.
4—Restriction at main jet.
5—Damaged nozzle.
6—Worn throttle shaft.
7—Air horn assembly loose.

Hard Starting with Engine Warm

1—Loose metering or defective discharge jets.
2—Defective jet gaskets.
3—Insufficient throttle opening at carburetor.

Lack of Power and Speed

1—Throttle valve out of adjustment. Not fully open when foot throttle is depressed to floor board.
2—Choke not opening fully.
3—If an auxiliary needle valve is used in a carburetor it might not seat properly when the choke is wide open.
4—Clogged main or bypass jets.
5—Improper float level.
6—Water or dirt in the float chamber.
7—Interrupted flow of fuel to the carburetor.
8—Air valve sticking (air valve type of carburetor).
9—*See also* Engine Hesitates when Accelerating and Ignition System.

Engine Hesitates when Accelerating

1—Choke valve not fully open. The result is an excessively rich mixture that is slow burning. If the carburetor has an auxiliary needle, make sure that this seats when the choke is wide open.
2—Too much accelerating will discharge, especially in summer, or a lack of fuel in the winter. Pump might be inoperative. Make sure water or dirt does not collect in the pump or its passages.
3—Vapor lock due to the use of high-test fuel in hot weather. Boiling of the fuel in the system can cause gas pockets in the vacuum tank, fuel pump, fuel lines or the carburetor. This results in an interrupted supply of fuel and causes hesitation when accelerating. A high-opening thermostat in the cooling system affects certain grades of fuel. This condition is sometimes defined as a *flat spot* when accelerating.
4—Flexible portion of fuel line on some installations collapses to lean mixture.

Engine Stalls on Sudden Throttle Opening

1—Mixture too lean.
2—Air leaks at throttle shaft, manifold, or carburetor joints.
3—Partially clogged fuel jets.
4—Fuel supply to the carburetor is not constant.
5—On air valve carburetors, weak auxiliary air valve spring or air valve stuck open.
6—Accelerator pump check valve sticking or leaking.
7—Step-up spring tension too weak.
8—Defective accelerator plunger.
9—Flexible portion of fuel line used on some installations collapses to lean mixture.

Accelerator Sticks

1—Loose pin in accelerating pump shaft.
2—Linkage not properly adjusted.

Engine Will Idle, but Will Not Accelerate

1—Loose high-speed carburetor jet.

Engine "Coughs" at Steady Driving Speeds

1—Worn main jet or metering rod.

Engine Lopes

1—Black, carbon-like deposit formed in carburetor throat restricting air bleed holes.

Engine Sluggish Caused by Slow Warm Up

1—Accumulation of carbon in heat riser of intake manifold.
2—Damper valve shaft sticking in bushings.
3—Defective thermostat in heat control.

Automatic Heat Control Stuck

1—Binding in shaft and bushing.
2—Thermostat coil wound too tight (has taken permanent set).
3—Counterweight lever loose on shaft.

Hissing Noise or Power Roar in Carburetor

1—A hissing sound and a power roar are natural with proper carburetor adjustment. Both can only be eliminated by fitting an intake silencer.

Vibrating Noise in Air Cleaner

1—Air cleaner not properly mounted (probably down too far).

Whistle in Carburetor Equipped with Oil Bath Air Cleaner

1—Filter plate in air cleaner upside down.

Smoky Exhaust

1—More generally evident with vacuum fuel feed system and is due to air vent of vacuum tank being clogged. Remove this unit from tank and blow on the threaded part removed from tank. If this does not open the vent, soak in cleaning solution or replace unit with a new one.
2—Air cleaner clogged permitting rich mixture.

Engine Will Not Idle without Roll with Proper Carburetor Adjustment

1—Can be caused by defective vacuum tank valves or clogged jets and fuel passages in carburetor. Clean carburetor thoroughly and check jets to maker's specifications.

Carburetor Noise

1—Air cleaner mounting loose.
2—Poppet valve in choke valve not seating.
3—Loose deflector tube in intake manifold to cylinder flange. Noise similar to tappet click.
4—Whistling noise; filter plate in air cleaner installed upside down.

See also Back Firing or Popping in Carburetor.
See also Hissing Noise or Power Roar.

Slopping of Gasoline at Tank Filler Neck

1—Air trapped over gasoline expanding and forcing out fuel.

Punctured or Logged Float

1—Indicated by mixture being too rich at all low speeds.

Gum Forms in Fuel

1—Due to high atmospheric temperature. Worse in summer or in heated building during winter.
2—Intimate contact with air. Supply in tank maintained at too low a level. When draining system for storage, draining must be complete; this includes fuel pump and carburetor.
3—Bright copper and soldering fluxes, when present, accelerate formation of gum.

Note: Acetone or half benzol and half alcohol are gum solvents.
Note: Improper carburetor adjustment can result if the carburetor is adjusted with the air cleaner and silencer removed. This could cause the engine to "lope" at low speed. When adjustment is made with cleaner and silencer removed, allowance should be made for the additional resistance to air flow this unit creates. Otherwise the mixture will be slightly rich.

Exhaust Gas Analysis.

1—High heat conductivity indicated. Rich mixture.
2—Low heat conductivity indicated. Lean mixture.

AUTOMATIC CHOKE CONTROL

Delco-Remy on Buick, Oldsmobile, and others.

Mixture Too Rich or Too Lean

1—Improper setting of initial closing temperatures. Control rod too long (mixture rich). Control rod too short (mixture lean).

Lean Mixture on Acceleration

1—Leaking or stuck valve in top of accelerating piston.

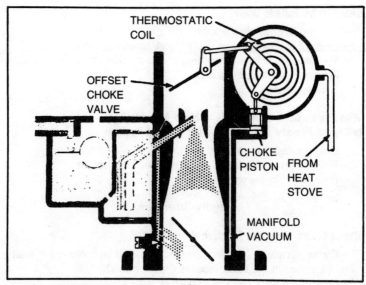

Automatic choke control.

Opening of Choker Fly after Starting not Correct

1—Moving parts binding.
2—Metering pin not set for proper timing of bellows movement.
3—Loose metering pin lock nut.
4—Defective gasket between control and heat riser.
5—Vacuum hole in riser obstructed or leaking.
6—Bellows not holding vacuum.

Engine Fails to Start

1—Engine flooded with raw fuel.
2—Vacuum fails to release choke.
3—Vacuum channels plugged.
4—Improper bellows metering pin timing.
5—*See* Mixture too Rich or too Lean.

Control Lever Fails to Return to Closed Position

1—Valve in top of accelerating piston not opening.

Popping or Spitting in Carburetor

1—Volatility selector not properly adjusted for fuel used.

Choke Does Not Return to Original Position with Throttle Closed

1—Binding or sticking pistons.

Choke Valve Fails to Open

1—Vacuum passage obstructed.
2—Leakage at choke gasket due to loose mounting bolts.
3—Vacuum leak around screw plug in end of "take-off" cylinder due to looseness or damaged gasket.
4—Sticking pistons.

With Engine Cold, Choke Fails to Move Momentarily to Closed Position and then Assume Original Position

1—Sluggish dash-pot piston.
2—Weak or broken dash-pot piston pull-out lever spring.
3—Binding in moving parts.

Bendix-Stromberg

Choke Control Does Not Function

1—Carburetor choke lever not properly adjusted on choke valve shaft.
2—Operating linkage binds (does not move freely).
3—Control rod not free in wide open or closed position.
4—Backlash in hook-up too great.
5—Choke lever not properly set in relation to unlocking cam.
6—Air cleaner interfering with carburetor choke lever.
7—Choke control hold-down bolts not drawn down evenly permitting air leakage.
8—Vacuum piston sticking.
9—Defective gasket between choke unit and manifold. No vacuum to trip kick lever or leakage prevents holding vacuum piston down.
10—Thermostat not properly aligned at zero marking.
11—Thermostat not adjusted at proper temperature (70 degrees Fahrenheit).

Sisson

Choke Control Does Not Function

1—Poor electrical connection between choke control and starter switch.
2—Poor electrical connection between choke control case and lockout pole shoe.
3—Loose connections or backlash in linkage.
4—Choke valve not properly adjusted on choke valve shaft.
5—Dirt or oil on electromagnet.
6—Oil around choke shaft or on operating mechanism. Unit must not be lubricated.
7—Armature pole to shoe clearance not correct (should be .015").
8—Clearance between choke lever and cam stop not correct (should be .015").

9—Poor ground connection between choke and manifold causing hard starting.

Engine Starts Hard

1—Choke valve sticking open.
2—Choke linkage sticking.
3—Choke piston sticking.

Poor Fuel Economy

1—Choke valve sticking closed or partly closed.
2—Choke linkage sticking.
3—Choke piston sticking.

Carter Climatic Control

Sluggish Action

1—Choke control not properly adjusted. Engine must be cold. Adjusting temperature 70 degrees Fahrenheit.
2—Choke valve not in proper alignment causing choke to stick in closed position or drag on air horn throughout range.
3—Thermostat coil tampered with (replace).
4—Air leaks due to defective gasket between piston plate housing and air horn.
5—Air leaks at flexible tube mounting.
6—Piston plate and gasket slots not in alignment.
7—Dirt in thermostatic coil housing. Use air pressure only to clean.
8—Port in port plate or passage through carburetor clogged with dirt.
9—Misalignment of parts in assembling.

Cold Engine Loads During Warm-up

1—Adjustment too rich. Turn choke housing clockwise one notch at a time to lean out. Low grades of fuel have tendency to run rich during warm-up.

Cold Engine Runs Lean During Warm-up

1—Adjustment too lean. Turn housing counterclockwise one notch at a time to richen adjustment. High-test fuels have a tendency to run lean during warm-up.

Choke Valve Will Not Open

1—Screen in housing clogged.
2—Piston binding in its cylinder.

Slow Warm-up on Cold Days

1—Excessive cooling of climatic control (deflect air stream from fan).

Excessive Carburetor Adjustment
Required for Smooth Idling During Warm-up

1—Dirt restricting air intake of control manifold, stove, or flexible tubing.

2—Air leak in flexible tubing or around flexible tubing at climatic control.

3—Dirt in screen in control housing.

SUPERCHARGER

Engine Will Not Hold Speed and Power

1—Drive belts slipping.

2—Blower rotor loose on shaft.

3—Air leaks between supercharger and manifold.

4—Defective oil seal in supercharger permitting air and oil to pass to engine.

5—Cracked supercharger housing.

6—Brakes dragging.

7—Chassis stiff.

8—Wrong jets in carburetor.

9—Restricted air cleaner.

10—Leaks or restrictions in fuel lines.

11—Fuel pump defective; engine starved for want of fuel at high speed.

12—Vapor lock in fuel lines.

13—High back pressure from exhaust system.

14—Valves float. Valve springs too weak.

15—Defective ignition coil. Breaks down at high speed.

16—Condenser capacity not suited to engine. Try lower capacity.

17—Breaker points bouncing at high speeds.

18—Automatic advance mechanism sticking.

19—Spark plugs defective or not properly gapped.

FUEL SYSTEM

No adjustment can be made on fuel pumps. A simple test is to assemble a line about 3 feet long to the inlet of the pump. By placing the end of this line in a tank of fuel and manipulating the rocker arm, observe whether there is suction and pressure. Another test is to disconnect the carburetor line, step on the starter, and observe whether fuel spurts out of the pump outlet. A simple test for suction and pressure is to hold your fingers over the inlet and outlet of the pump, and then manipulate the rocker arm. When reinstalling the pump or when the bowl is removed for cleaning, check by watching the priming action of the pump. Pumps should prime themselves—the bowl should fill—when the starter is depressed in about 20 seconds or less.

MECHANICAL PUMP
Lack of Gasoline

1—Broken, split, or clogged fuel line.

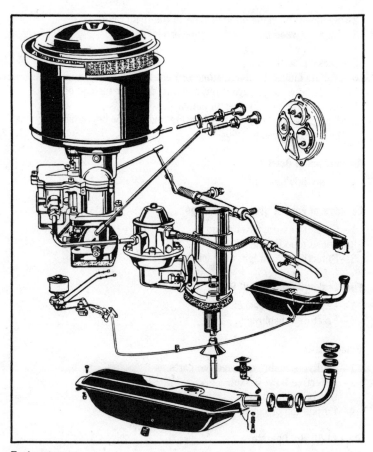

Fuel system.

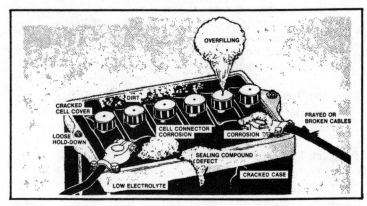

Battery.

2—Sediment blocking off standpipe in the main tank.

3—Line between pump and carburetor clogged.

4—Float needle passage clogged.

5—Leaky pipe fittings permitting air to enter fuel line.

6—Tubing kinked by flying stone or bent to shut off flow.

7—Glass bowl loose permitting pump to draw air instead of fuel.

8—Dirty screen or strainer in pump.

9—Defective bowl gasket. Bowl gasket must not be dry or hard and must lay flat on its seat.

Air Bubbles in Bowl

1—Leaky bowl gasket.

Leakage of Fuel at Diaphragm Flange

1—Careless assembly of pump.

2—Loose pipe fittings.

3—Defective diaphragm or diaphragm gasket.

Fuel Leakage Around Pull Rod

1—Leaky pull rod gasket.

2—Fractured diaphragm.

Pump Leaks

1—Faulty assembly or defective parts.

2—Defective bowl gasket.

3—Defective diaphragm.

4—Porous top or cover.

Pump Will Not Operate

1—Punctured or worn out diaphragm.

2—Broken diaphragm spring.

3—Defective or wrong type linkage; linkage becomes locked.

4—Sticky valves or springs caused by gum in fuel.

5—Valves warped, dirty, or not seating.

6—Defective valve springs.

Carburetor Flooding

1—*See* Carburetor Floods.

2—Pump air dome not of proper size.

Pump Cuts Out on High Speed and Long Pull

1—Loose connections in piping.

2—Loose valve seat.

3—Warped valves.

4—Air leaks in line or pump.

5—Air dome needed to supply proper amount of fuel.

6—Fuel boiling in line and pump; insulate pump from heat and install fuel line outside of frame.

Stalling and Failure to Pump at Low Speeds

1—Pump does not hold pressure due to defective valves or other parts.

2—Defective pump cover or top.

3—Leaks around glass bowl.

4—Leaks in fuel line.

Pump Noisy in Operation

1—Broken rocker arm spring.

2—Rocker arm bent or binding on shaft.

3—Pull rod linkage or connections binding.

4—Rocker arm not following eccentric on camshaft.

Pump Quits at Times

1—Dirt in fuel line.

2—Defective valves.

3—Loose valve seats.

4—Sticking pull rod.

5—Binding linkage or rocker arm.

ANALYSIS OF VACUUM PUMP TROUBLES

Vacuum Pump Will Not Operate

1—Defect in windshield wiper (defective valves and fittings).

2—Defective pump valves.

3—Defective pump diaphragm.

High Gas Pressure or Noise in Pump

1—Lack of clearance for pump parts.

2—Fuel pump link striking upper diaphragm protector.

3—Pump and rocker arm pit worn.

4—Diaphragm spring of vacuum pump rubbing on fiber bushing.

Note: When making a vacuum test at fuel pump, with gauge located at pump intake, a reading of 10 developed with engine idling should require 1 minute for the needle to drop to zero after the engine is stopped. A faster drop indicates poor condition of pump intake valve.

ELECTRIC FUEL PUMP

The following main causes of trouble with the Stewart-Warner electric fuel pump might require diagnosis. Make an installation test. Check for current between the vehicle frame and the positive wire connection to the top of the pump. When current is found here, ground a clean surface of the pump to a clean, scraped portion of the vehicle frame. If pump now operates, the pump base is not in good metallic contact with the car frame. If the pump fails to operate, it indicates troubles within the pump.

Failure to Deliver Sufficient Fuel

1—Air leaks at sediment bowl gasket.
2—Cracked fuel line or leaks at fittings.
3—Carburetor line too small or restricted fittings.
4—Pump not properly located.
5—Poor electrical connections or low battery voltage.
6—Leaks in supply line.
7—Clogged delivery or suction line.
8—Weak plunger spring.
9—Worn piston rings in pump.
10—Sticking piston.
11—Leaks at valves.
12—Foreign matter or dirt in pump.

Failure to Supply any Fuel

1—Pump might be inoperative. See above.
2—Binding or sticking piston.
3—Open circuit through pump.
4—Coil spring might not exert necessary slight pressure on spring retainer.
5—Broken wires at coil terminal.
6—Foreign matter on face of armature and top of plunger.
7—Pump short-circuited.
8—Cracked insulators or improper assembly.

Pump Will Not Shut off

1—Piston continues to stroke when engine is stopped.
2—Leaks at piston or valves.

VACUUM TANKS

Stewart-Warner leverless tank. *See also* Lever Type Tank.

Failure to Draw Fuel

1—Air leaks in vacuum line or fittings. Loose or broken fittings at vacuum tank, manifold, or main supply tank.
2—Clogged main tank vent.
3—Restriction in fuel line.
4—Atmospheric vent not seating.

Over Rich Mixture Flooding Engine

1—Leaky float in vacuum tank.
2—Upper float stem rubs on side of tank.

Fuel Does Not Flow or Flows Slowly to Carburetor

1—Clogged vent to inner shell or clogged vent tube in vacuum tank.
2—Sticking flapper valve.
3—Valve tripping might be sluggish.

Gasoline Flows from Vent Hole or Pipe

1—Vent hole in filler cap of main tank clogged.
2—Vehicle standing with fuel level in main tank higher than vacuum tank. Fuel draining by gravity.

Electrical Systems and Switches

INSTRUMENT PANEL GAUGES

On the instrument panel are found various types of gauges, registering oil pressure, gasoline, oil and water levels. Some of these operate electrically, some hydrostatically, and others are just plain pressure gauges.

Electric Oil Pressure Gauge

Erratic Action:
1—Defective engine unit.
Not Registering Accurately:
1—Defective engine unit.
Registers with Switch "On"; Engine not Running
1—Short-circuit in wiring or gauge unit. Usually results in burning out of unit (necessitating replacement).

Pressure-Type oil Gauge

Gauge Failure
1—Accumulation of oxide in small hole at gauge connection. Clean with wire.

Gasoline Gauge (Electric Type)
Gauge Does Not Register with Ignition Switch "On"

1—Break in line between dash unit and ignition switch.
2—Poor ground at tank or gauge unit.

Gauge Registers Empty under All Conditions

1—Break in line between dash unit and ignition switch.
2—No ground or poor ground at tank unit.

Gauge Registers Full under All Conditions

1—Short in tank unit or tank unit line.
2—Reversed wires on dash unit.
3—No ground or poor ground at dash or tank units.

Gauge Reverses Readings

1—Reversed connections on dash unit. Also on tank unit when this has two terminals.

Overreading

1—Bimetal-type; if car is radio equipped, tank unit condenser "shorted."

Spasmodic or Erratic Reading

1—Dirty contacts.
2—Binding or sluggish action of tank float.

AUTO-LITE GASOLINE GAUGE
1939 Chrysler, DeSoto, Dodge, and Plymouth

Gauge Reads Empty with Tank Full

1—Blue and brown wires connected between dash and tank units reversed.

Gauge Reads Full with Tank Empty

1—Blue and brown wires connected between dash and tank units reversed.

Inaccurate Readings

1—Nuts attaching wiring to terminals at back of dash unit drawn up too tight. Gauge must be replaced.

Sticking Pointers

1—Insufficient clearance between lower end or pointer and panel. Insert paper gasket between mounting face and back of panel.
2—Any other condition requires replacement of unit.

Fluctuating Pointer

1—Dirty contact points in dash unit.

Tank Condition	Blue Wire Grounded	Brown Wire Grounded	Blue Wire Open	Brown Wire Open
Empty	Empty	½ full	½ full	Empty
½ full	¼ full	¾ full	Full	Empty
Full	½ full	Full	Full	Empty

Electric-Type Oil Level Gauge

This type of gauge operates on the same principle as the electric-type oil pressure gauge and the same methods for diagnosis apply.

Electric-Type Water Level Gauge

This type of gauge operates on the same principle as the electric type oil pressure gauge and the same methods for diagnosis apply.

Hydrostatic Gauge

Gauge Reading too High:
   1—Too much liquid in U-tube.
   2—Wrong kind of liquid in U-tube.
   3—For the dial type, gauge is defective. It has been overpressured in testing.

Gauge Reading too Low
   1—Improper liquid in U-tube.
   2—Not enough liquid in U-tube.

Unsteady Reading:
   1—Not enough air entering main tank; filler cap vent clogged.
   2—Vent hole in tank unit clogged with water or sediment.
   3—Gasoline in air line.
   4—When connected with vacuum tank, improper operation of vacuum tank.

No Reading or Reading Drops:
   1—Leak in air line or tank unit.
   2—Leak in gauge head.

AMMETER

When analyzing electrical trouble, keep in mind that the electrical system comprises a number of units and each is subject to trouble in time. Essentially, it is necessary to first arrive at some conclusion as to the possible location of the trouble, but more generally this is indicated by the nature of the trouble. Testing equipment is necessary in most cases. Nevertheless, there are instances where trouble is accidentally located without equipment. The most satisfactory method is to make continuity tests and take current readings. Otherwise you will grope in the dark. Each of the component units of the electrical system has been analyzed separately to make the analysis complete.

Ammeter Does Not Show Generator Charging

   1—Generator armature or field grounded (open or short-circuited).
   2—Weak brush springs.
   3—Brush holder grounded or binds on post.

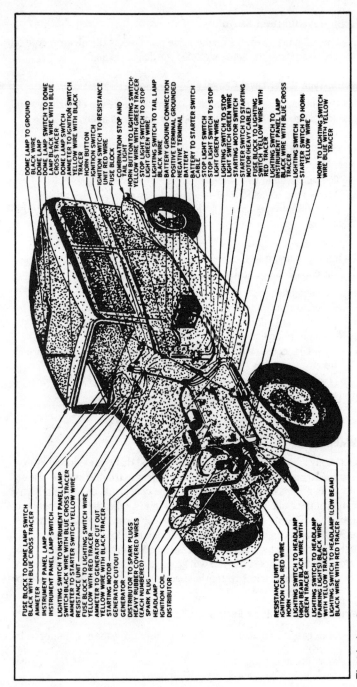

Electrical system.

4—Relay points dirty. Not properly adjusted or sticking.

5—Relay base not grounded or open in circuit.

6—Winding shorted. Grounded or open in circuit.

7—Terminals or connections not tight, corroded, rusty, or clips unsoldered.

8—Wiring grounded, shorted, or open circuit from generator to ammeter, to starter switch, to battery, to ground.

9—*See also* Needle Sticks and Ammeter Burned Out.

No Reading at High Speed

1—Brush springs weak or broken.

2—Commutator out of round.

3—Brushes worn short.

4—Flying ground (shorts or opens in armature).

Unsteady Reading

1—Polarity reversed causing relay points to vibrate.

2—Weak brush springs or brushes worn short.

3—Arcing due to poorly seated brushes.

4—Brush holder sticks.

5—Belt driven generator; belt slipping.

6—Poor connections in charging circuit.

7—Poor connections inside generator.

8—Loose commutator segment in generator.

9—*See also* Ammeter does not Show Generator Charging

Ammeter Shows Discharge with Switch "Off"

1—Circuit breaker points stick.

2—Circuit breaker points set too close.

3—Circuit breaker spring weak.

4—Partial short between ammeter and circuit breaker or between switch and ammeter.

5—Ignition button in.

Ammeter Charge Reading Drops Abruptly when Engine Is Warm

1—Condition normal due to thermostat opening.

Ammeter Shows Charge with Engine Stopped and Lights Burning

1—Wiring connections reversed at ammeter.

2—Polarity of battery changed.

Ammeter Burned Out

1—Excessive charge due to a short-circuit in ammeter to switch wire, switch to lamp wires, or switch to horn wire that melted solder or burned out wires.

Ammeter Needle Goes beyond Last Mark on Discharge Scale

1—Relay points stuck.
2—Loose connections.
3—Short circuit.
4—Ground.

Ammeter Needle Bent

1—Excessive current throws needle against stop.
2—Broken glass permitting damage to needle.

Ammeter Needle Sticks

1—Needle rubs on dial.
2—Ammeter bearings bind.

GENERATOR
Charging Rate Low or Unsteady

1—Battery terminals loose or corroded.
2—Brushes worn or broken.
3—Weak or broken brush springs. Arcing at brushes.
4—Brush or holder sticking.
5—Commutator dirty.
6—High mica between commutator segments.
7—Commutator out-of-round.
8—Drive belt slipping.
9—Commutator segments worn, cut, or loose.
10—Improper adjustment of third brush.
11—Battery plates sulphated.
12—Thermostat resistance burned out.
13—Cut-out relay contacts not closing.
14—Field coils loose.
15—Field coils broken.
16—Cut-out leads loose.
17—Armature weak.

Charging Rate Low or Zero

1—Dirty or greasy commutator.
2—Commutator out-of-round.
3—High mica between commutator segments.
4—Brush spring grounded.
5—Drive belt slipping or broken.
6—Thermostat does not close.
7—Armature binds.
8—Armature shaft bent.
9—Lead broken.
10—Shorted armature.

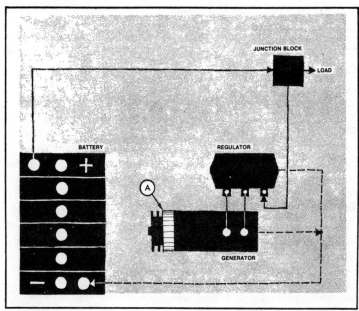

Generator.

11—Open armature.
12—Grounded armature.
13—Large part of field winding shorted.
14—Grounded field.
15—Open field.
16—Field burned out.
17—Field coil reversed.

Generator Overheats

1—High resistance in charging circuit.
2—Excessive charging rate.
3—Partially grounded brush ring.
4—Grounded brush rings.
5—Damaged armature or field coil.

Generator Noisy

1—Bearings worn or broken.
2—Excessive end play in armature shaft. Might sound like knock in engine.
3—Armature shaft sprung.
4—Armature rubs or binds.
5—Loose poles.

6—Pole pieces too close to armature.

7—Thrown windings.

8—Unit not properly assembled.

Charging Rate Too High

1—Generator third brush improperly adjusted.

2—Thermostat does not open.

Generator Cuts Out under Speed

1—Due to centrifugal or flying short in armature winding.

2—Due to poor connection in armature circuit that is shorted under centrifugal force due to speed or armature.

Generator Dead (as Shown by Ammeter)

1—Commutator dirty.

2—Brushes sticking in holders or broken.

3—Battery terminals loose, broken, or corroded.

4—Cut-out points stuck open.

5—Loose connections in cut-out.

6—Armature winding insulation defective.

7—Armature burned out or connections loose.

8—Generator to ammeter wire broken or burned out.

Generator Loose on Mounting

1—Frequently caused by an unbalanced drive pulley setting up vibration.

2—Fan belt tension too heavy.

Sparking at Brushes

1—Imperfect brush contact.

2—Brushes worn or broken.

3—Brushes sticking in holders.

4—Faulty brush fitting.

5—Brush setting wrong.

6—Weak brush spring tension.

7—Brushes of wrong material.

8—Dirt or grease on commutator.

9—High mica between commutator segments.

10—Loose segment in commutator.

11—Commutator segments worn or cut.

12—Commutator out-of-round.

Generator Brushes Noisy

1—Commutator rough.

2—Improper fitting of brushes.

3—Brush holder spring weak or broken.

4—High mica between commutator segments.
5—Loose commutator segment.
6—Hard spot on brush.
7—Loose brush holder.
8—Spring tension too great.
9—Brushes not of proper material.

Commutator Brushes

1—Soft, oily, or wrong type of commutator glazed or blackened. Generator will not charge until relay contacts are closed by hand.
2—Weak brush spring. Charging rate too low or unsteady. Arcing at brushes.
3—Brush ring grounded. With dead generator ground generator will not charge. With partial ground, generator will overheat and appear to have a shorted armature.
4—Brush holder sticking. Low or unsteady output. Similar to weak brush spring.

Brushes Worn

1—Brushes soft.
2—Improper brush setting.
3—Brush springs too stiff.
4—Commutator rough.
5—High mica between commutator segments.
6—Loose commutator segment.

Brushes Soft or Oily

1—Brushes have been lubricated.
2—Excessive lubrication of commutator end bearing.
3—Wrong type brushes.

Brush Spring

1—Weak. Charging rate low or unsteady. Arcing at brushes.

Brush Holders Stick

1—Box type. Dirty or gummy brush or damaged holder.
2—Hinge type. Bent or rusted brush holder.

Brush Ring

1—Partial ground. Generator overheats.
2—Dead ground. Generator short-circuited.

Brush Ring Grounded

1—Broken or burned insulation.
2—Metal chips, dirt, or carbon dust under brush ring.

Commutator

1—High mica. Charging rate low or unsteady. Arcing and burning of brushes.
2—Glazed or blackened. Brushes soft or oily.
3—Commutator out-of-round. Generator stops charging or charges unsteady at high speed.
4—Dirty or greasy. Generator will not charge until relay contacts have been closed by hand.
5—Third brush advanced too far (throwing solder).
6—Thermostat contacts not opening (throwing solder).

Commutator Dirty or Greasy

1—Excessive lubrication of commutator end bearing.
2—Brushes not of proper type.

Commutator Cut

1—Brushes too hard.
2—Brush spring too stiff.
3—Brush spring broken.
4—Brushes worn or broken.

Internal Open Circuit

1—Gummy commutator.
2—Brushes worn or not properly seated.
3—Weak brush springs.
4—Brush arms sticking.
5—High mica on commutator.
6—Solder thrown from armature.
7—Loose internal connections at generator or third brush arm.
8—Defective relay.

Field Coils

1—Shorted. Damaged or defective insulation. Charging rate low or zero.
2—Grounded. In effect, the same as a short-circuit. Insulation worn or broken.
3—Open circuit. Generator will not charge under any condition.
4—Field coil burned out. Generator will not charge under any condition.
5—Field coil reversed. Output low or zero. Field current normal. Generator motors in direction opposite to normal.

Field Coils Shorted

1—Defective or damaged insulation.
2—Field coils pinched at assembly.

Field Coils Grounded

1—Insulation worn or broken.
2—Metal particles between field coil and frame or pole. Same as shorted field on grounded system.

Field Coils Open

1—Connections unsoldered or broken.

Field Coils Burned Out

1—Loose connections at ammeter.
2—Loose connections at cutout.
3—Battery terminals loose or corroded.
4—Generator or starting motor ground connections loose.
5—Cut-out wire loose at generator.
6—Generator operated on open circuit or high resistance in circuit.

Field Coil Reversed

1—Improper assembly or connections.

Poles Loose

1—Retaining screws loose or broken.

Polarity Reversed

1—Battery connections reversed.
2—Generator polarity reversed during test.

End Play in Armature

1—Bearing caps too tight.
2—Bearings broken or worn.
3—Thrust bearing face worn.
4—Worn thrust washer.
5—Thrust washer omitted.
6—Driving gears improperly assembled.
7—Oil thrower loose on shaft.

Armature Binding Cord Broken

1—Field coils loose.
2—Brush holder broken.

Shorted Armature

1—Armature heats. Solder melts from commutator.
2—Insulation burned. Wires in contact with each other.
3—Metal chips between commutator bars.

Open Circuited Armature

1—Low or zero charging rate.
2—Commutator burned at bars connected to open circuit.

Grounded Armature

1—Armature heats. Wires in contact with shaft laminations due to damaged or defective insulation.

Sprung Armature Shaft

1—Noisy generator.
2—Bearings heat or burn out.

Armature Binds or Rubs

1—Generator noisy.
2—Worn shaft bearings.
3—Armature does not rotate freely.
4—Loose pole.
5—Improperly assembled.

Laminations Scored

1—Poles loose.

Armature Heats

1—See armature shorted or grounded.

Bearings Heat or Burn Out

1—Armature shaft bent or sprung.
2—Generator noisy.

Worn or Damaged Bearings

1—Dirt or grit in bearings.
2—Excessive load due to tight drive belt.
3—Armature not rotating freely.
4—Excessive end play in armature shaft.
5—Grounded armature.

Thermostat

1—Does not open. Charging rate continuously high.
2—Does not close. Charging rate continuously low.
3—Dirty thermostat contacts. Reverse field lead and attach to ground. With open points, charging rate will increase.
4—Burned out resistance. Normal charging while cold; stops when hot.

Cut-Out Closes Late

1—Low voltage.
2—Air gap too large.
3—Spring tension too great.
4—Partial ground or short in shunt coil.
5—Armature movement sluggish due to friction.

Cut-Out Closes Early

1—High voltage.
2—Weak spring tension.
3—Air gap too small.

Cut-Out Fails to Close

1—Low voltage.
2—Excessive spring tension.
3—Air gap too large.
4—Armature locked by friction.
5—Loose connection, short, or ground in shunt coil.

Cut-Out Fails to Open

1—Spring broken.
2—Weak spring tension.
3—Armature stuck.

Cut-Out Vibrates

1—Shunt or series coil reversed.
2—Wrong battery polarity.
3—Intermittent short in shunt coil.

Cut-Out Relay

1—Voltage coil open. Points do not close.
2—Open current coil. No current to battery.
3—Out of adjustment.
4—Contacts chatter and arc. Polarity reversed.
5—Cuts in too soon. Ammeter indicates discharge after points close. Points might chatter. Improper adjustment of armature tension; spring weak.
6—Cuts in too late. Charging current too high after relay closes. Improper adjustment or too much spring tension.
7—Cuts out too soon. Contacts separate before current has dropped to zero. Improper adjustment.
8—Cuts out too late. Improper adjustment or armature spring loose or broken.

9—Open shunt. Winding field fuse, thermostat resistance, or field winding burned out.

10—Shorted shunt. Field fuse, thermostat resistance, or field winding burned out.

11—Open series winding. Loose connections or broken wire.

12—Shorted series winding. Contact points chatter. Damaged or defective insulation.

13—Grounded windings. On grounded system, same effect as shorted windings. Damaged or defective insulation.

14—Contacts burned. Cuts out too late. Relay action erratic. Reversed polarity causing chatter.

Dirty Circuit Breaker

1—Cover missing.

2—Dirt between contacts.

3—Dirt in core and armature.

4—Careless handling.

Circuit Breaker Does Not Close

1—Generator dead.

2—Loose connections at circuit breaker, generator, or ground.

3—Circuit breaker armature stuck.

4—Circuit breaker spring too stiff.

5—Circuit breaker shunt open.

Circuit Breaker Vibrates

1—Short in lighting circuit.

GENERATOR REGULATION

Third Brush Type

1—Output too high. Third brush too near main brush.

2—Output too low. Third brush too far from main brush.

Current Regulated Shunt Type

1—Output too high. Spring tension on current regulator too high.

2—Output too low. Spring tension on current regulator too low.

Voltage and Current Regulation

1—Control relay opening voltage. Decrease armature spring tension to decrease voltage. Increase armature spring tension to increase voltage.

2—Control relay closing voltage. Increase voltage by increasing armature air gap. Decrease voltage by decreasing armature air gap.

Voltage Regulation Generator Not Charging

1—Regulator base has poor ground.
2—Open circuit between field terminals on generator and voltage regulator.
3—Generator dead.
4—Regulator points oxidized.

Voltage Regulation: Charging Rate Always Too High

1—Battery defective.
2—Regulator set for too high a voltage.

Voltage Regulation: Charging Rate Always Too Low

1—Battery defective or sulphated.
2—High resistance between regulator and battery.
3—Defective voltage regulator.
4—Regulator points oxidized.

Generator Will Not Deliver Set Output

1—Regulator points burnt or dirty (causing high resistance).

Voltage Regulator Points Burn

1—Dust particles between points.

Oxidation of Regulator Points

1—Radio bypass condenser mounted on field terminal of generator or regulator (vibrating-type regulator)

Damaged Voltage Regulator

1—Generator run or voltage regulator set with regulator "BAT." wire disconnected.

Excessive Sparking and Erratic Operation of Voltage Regulator

1—Low tension on upper contact spring.
2—Misalignment of contacts.
3—Oxidized points causing high resistance.
4—Radio bypass condenser connected to field terminal of regulator causing oxidized points.
5—Misalignment of contacts.
6—Low tension on upper spring.

AUTO-LITE VR SERIES REGULATOR
No Control of Voltage

1—Open voltage regulator shunt coil.
2—Sticking voltage regulator points.

3—Stationary contact point grounded to yoke.
4—Field terminal grounded.
5—Field terminal to regulator contact point grounded.

Improper Control of Voltage

1—Shorted voltage regulator shunt coil.

Excessive Fluctuation of Ammeter

1—Dirty or high-resistance voltage regulator points.
2—Sticking voltage regulator points.
3—Broken regulator resistor.
4—Wrong regulator resistor.
5—Hinge on voltage regulator or current regulator not tight against arm.
6—Dirty or high-resistance current regulator points.
7—Low discharge amperage on opening of circuit breaker.
Note: The ammeter will fluctuate some just as the regulator points start to operate. This will decrease with a slight increase of generator speed if the regulator is OK.

Intermittent Operation of Circuit Breaker

1—Dirty or high-resistance voltage or current regulator points.
2—Sticking voltage regulator points.

Drop in Voltage as Voltage Regulator Starts to Operate

1—Sticking voltage regulator points.

High or Low Operating Voltage

1—Voltage regulator gap change.
2—Low or high voltage reading.
3—High resistance in voltage regulator shunt coil.

Improper Control at High Speeds

1—Broken regulator resistor.
2—Wrong regulator resistor.

No Charge

1—Low voltage setting.
2—Current regulator series coil open.
3—Dirty circuit breaker points.
4—Burnt circuit breaker points.
5—Open series coil in circuit breaker.
6—Grounded terminal.
7—Grounded circuit breaker.
8—Improper circuit breaker core gap.
9—Closing voltage too high.

Improper Charge Rate (High)

1—High voltage setting.
2—High resistance in voltage regulator shunt coil.
3—Current regulator series coil shorted.
4—Current regulator gap change.
5—Sticking current regulator points.
6—Current regulator stationary contact grounded to yoke.
7—High current setting.

Improper Charge Rate (Low)

1—Current regulator gap change.
2—Low current setting.
3—High resistance of points.

No Control of Output

1—Field terminal grounded.
2—Lead from field terminal on regulator to contact point grounded.
3—Current regulator stationary contact grounded to yoke.
4—Current regulator yoke grounded to base.

Circuit Breaker Inoperative

1—Shorted shunt winding.
2—Open shunt winding.

High Discharge with Engine Dead and No Load

1—Sticking circuit breaker points.
2—Improper core gap of circuit breaker.

Continuous High Discharge

1—Grounded battery terminal.
2—Grounded stationary contact support in circuit breaker.

Circuit Breaker Operation Erratic

1—Improper core gap.
2—Hinge on reverse.
3—Armature not floated.

Circuit Breaker Points Flutter

1—Closing voltage too low.
2—Low discharge amperage on opening of circuit breaker.
3—Opening on charge.

Indicator or Telltale Light Will Not Operate

1—Flasher contact circuit open.

Indicator or Telltale Light Burns Continuously

1—Flasher contact circuit shorted.

Burnt Voltage or Current Regulator Points

1—Broken regulator resistor.
2—Wrong regulator resistor.

Circuit Breaker Points do not Close

1—Current regulator series coil open.
2—Shorted shunt winding.
3—Open shunt winding.
4—Open series coil in circuit breaker.
5—Grounded terminal.
6—Grounded circuit breaker.

BATTERY

Battery Cannot Be Maintained at Full Charge

1—Voltage regulator set lower than specified. Generator charging rate too low.

Discharged

1—Generator output low.
2—Excessive drain on battery when starting.
3—Terminals loose or corroded.
4—Internal short-circuit.
5—Plate connections to terminal strap broken.
6—Circuit breaker points stuck.
7—Short in wiring.
8—Defective wire insulation causing ground.
9—Polarity of one cell reversed.
10—Poor ground connection.
11—Short in or defective stop light switch.

Will Not Hold Charge

1—Low charging rate.
2—Electrolyte level low.
3—Excessive use of starter.
4—Too many electrical units for battery capacity.
5—Sediment in battery jars.

Battery Heats

1—Excessive charging rate.
2—Lack of water.
3—Undercharged for considerable time.

4—Sulphated plates.
5—Internal short-circuit or ground.
6—High discharge rate.
7—High internal resistance.

Battery Gases Rapidly

1—Excessive charging rate.
2—Electrolyte level low.
3—Sulphated plates.

Low Voltage

1—Internal short-circuit.
2—Polarity of cell reversed.

One Cell Requires More Water than Others

1—Leaking jar.
2—Short-circuited plates.

Cells Require Frequent Additions of Water

1—Charging rate too high.
2—Short-circuited plates.
3—Voltage control unit lacks sufficient range to properly protect the battery.

Battery Frozen

1—Battery discharged.
2—Excessive use of current.
3—Charging rate too low for winter requirements.

Low Gravity

1—Overcharging.
2—Overdischarging.
3—Spilling or slopping.
4—Leaky or broken jar.

High Gravity

1—Evaporation of water.
2—Unnecessary additions of acid.

Plate Sulphation

1—Eectrolyte level too low.
2—Overdischarging.
3—Standing in discharged condition.
4—Adding acid to replace evaporation.

5—Local action.
6—Battery permitted to gas violently or overheat.

Plates Buckling

1—Overcharged.
2—Overdischarged.
3—Overheating due to overcharging.
4—Sulphating.
5—Short-circuit.

Plates Shedding Active Material

1—Overcharging.
2—Overdischarging.
3—Long periods of idleness.
4—Age of battery.

Hardening of Active Material

1—Electrolyte level too low.
2—Plate exposure to air.
3—Long periods of idleness.
4—Age of battery.

Separators Worn Through

1—Natural wear.
2—Buckling of plates.

Separators Treeing

1—Natural growth of material.

Jar Leaking

1—Vibration.
2—Sudden shock.
3—Battery not held solid in place.

Leaks Acid

1—Electrolyte level too high.
2—Vent plugs obstructed.
3—Broken jar.
4—Battery cover broken.
5—Terminals loose in top plate.

Jar Broken

1—Vibration.
2—Sudden shock.

3—Battery not held solid in place.
4—Battery frozen.
5—Mishandling.

Connections and Terminals Broken or Corroded

1—Battery loose in mounting.
2—Corrosion due to slopping.
3—Defective lead burning.

Wood Case Rotted

1—Slopping.
2—Excessive gasing or boiling.

LIGHTING SYSTEM

Lamps Do Not Light

1—Bulbs burned out.
2—Fuses burned out.
3—Battery nearly or completely discharged.
4—Battery terminals loose, corroded, or broken.
5—Battery frozen.
6—Ammeter burned out.
7—Loose connections at lamps, switches, or generator.
8—Defective connectors at lamps.
9—Starting motor ground between battery and motor broken.
10—Broken wire or loose connection between battery and ammeter or ammeter and switch.
11—Circuit breaker contacts do not close, are not clean, or spring tension is not sufficient. If the circuit breaker vibrates, there is a short in the lighting circuit.
12—Metal contacts of switch worn or burned.

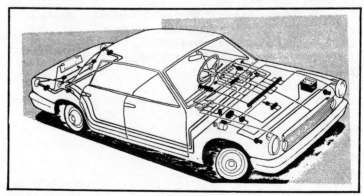

Lighting system.

Headlamps Burned Out

1—High voltage in circuit.
2—Battery terminals corroded.
3—Short in headlamp connector.
4—Loose connection at ammeter, battery, or starting motor.
5—Voltage regulator set higher than specified; generator constantly overcharging.
6—Sticking voltage regulator points.

New Bulbs Have Insufficient Candlepower

1—Dirty lenses.
2—Tarnished reflectors.
3—Poor connections.
4—Overloaded wiring.
5—Ineffective switches.
6—Ineffective fuses.
7—Ineffective fuse blocks.
8—Defective ammeter.
9—Defective ground connection at lamp.
10—Defective battery cable.
11—Defective battery ground cable.
12—Weak battery.

Lights Brighten when Engine Speed Is Increased

1—High resistance in lighting circuit. Location indicated by faulty connection being warm or hot.
2—High resistance in charging circuit.
3—Poor battery ground connection.
4—Poor connection between battery terminal and cable.
5—Overcharged battery.
6—Battery plates sulphated. High internal resistance.
7—Battery spiked with acid.
8—Loose mounting of cross member to which battery is grounded.
9—Loose reflector causing poor connection at lamp.
10—Poor ground between lamps and battery.
11—Headlamp bulb amperage too high. Candlepower of bulb too high.
12—High resistance in light switch.
13—Poor connections in lighting switch.
14—High and low beam regulator contacts corroded or poor tension on contact points.
15—Loose rivets in headlamp switch.
16—Poorly soldered connections inside ammeter.
17—Connections at ammeter reversed.
18—Loose rivets on fuse block.
19—Loose fuse holder.

20—Moisture in various parts of circuit setting up high resistance.
21—Soldered connections fluxed with acid (causing poor electrical contact).
22—Loose connections at soldered terminals. Few strands of wire carrying the current.
23—High resistance in wire from generator to ammeter; too small for current carried in the circuit.
24—Connections at starter switch loose or dirty.
25—Poor ground between generator and motor.
26—High resistance in generator cutout.
27—Cutout adjusted to cut in too late (loading the light circuit).
28—Voltage controls loose on mounting.
29—Improper adjustment of voltage regulator.
30—High voltage due to partially shorted generator fields.
31—Defective generator brush lead.
32—Defective generator brushes or mounting.

Lamps Burn Dim at All Times

1—High-voltage bulbs being used.
2—Lamps out of focus.
3—Battery nearly or completely discharged.
4—Short circuit in battery.
5—Polarity of cell reversed.
6—Battery frozen.
7—Blackened bulbs. Bulbs are old and worn out.
8—Loose connections on circuit breaker or between circuit breaker and lamps.
9—Dirt or corrosion on circuit breaker points.

Lamps Brighten when Engine Speed Is Increased

1—High-resistance in charging circuit.
2—Poor battery ground connection.
3—Improper adjustment of voltage regulator.

Lamps Flicker

1—Poor lamp grounds.
2—Loose reflector in lamps.
3—Battery terminals loose or corroded.
4—Defective lamp connectors.
5—Broken, dirty, or loose connections in switch.
6—Poor connections at ammeter, switch, or starting motor.
7—Battery electrolyte level low.
8—Rusty connections.
9—Late closing of generator cutout relay.
10—Defective resistor in voltage control.

Bulbs Short Lived

1—Low voltage bulbs used.
2—Charging rate of generator too high.
3—Battery terminals loose or corroded.
4—Battery electrolyte level low.
5—Loose connections in generator circuit.
6—Short-circuited plate in battery.
7—Inferior quality of bulb being used.

Smoky Bulbs

1—High voltage in circuit (in excess of bulb capacity).

Beams from Lamps Do Not Rise or Lower Together

1—Wrong connections at lamp sockets.
2—Wrong connections at connectors on frame.

Lamps Bright in Both Dim and Bright Positions

1—Dimmer resistance shorted.
2—Resistance wire burned or pressed together.
3—Insulation burned allowing ends of wire to come together.

No Control of Country Passing Beam

1—Inspect bulb for short between filaments causing both to burn.

Neither Headlamp Lights, (Switch in Bright Position)

1—Lamps burned out.
2—Poor connections between lamps and sockets.
3—Broken wire or loose connection between switch and lamps.
4—*See also* Lamps do not Light.

Lamps Do Not Light (Switch in Dim Position)

1—Dimmer resistance burned out.
2—Short or ground in lighting circuit.
3—Use of bulbs drawing more current than resistance was designed to carry.

One or More (Not All) Lights Fail

1—Poor bulb contact.
2—Defective bulb.
3—Loose connections at lamp which does not light.
4—Poor connections at terminal on switch that supplies current to lamp.

Lighting Switch Troubles

1—Turn on switch. If ammeter does not indicate discharge, look for an open circuit.

2—If no lamps burn through complete switch movement, the contacts on the relay are held open or internal switch connections are open.

3—If relay vibrates with switch on, there is a ground in the lamps or sockets. To locate, disconnect switch wires one at a time until relay stops vibrating.

Instrument and Tail Lamp Do Not Light

1—Bulb burned out (either dash or tail lamp bulb).
2—Poor tail lamp ground.
3—Poor connections between lamps and sockets.
4—Defective lamp connectors.
5—Broken wire or loose connection between lamp and switch.

Instrument Lamp Burned Out

1—Lamp grounded to instrument board.
2—Lead from tail lamp to lamp grounded.

Dome Light Burns Dim

1—Loose or corroded connections in the lamp circuit.
2—Generator charging rate too low for driver's requirements. The result is in an undercharged battery.

Headlamp Rattles

1—Headlamp lens loose.
2—Headlamp tie-rod broken or loose.
3—Headlamp or bracket loose.

Headlamp Glare

1—Bulbs not properly focused.
2—Mounting not in proper adjustment. Lamps not aimed properly.

Hazy or Tarnished Reflectors

1—Defective gasket back of lens permitting moisture to enter.

Thermo Circuit Breaker Vibrates

1—Short in one of the lighting circuits. Trace all circuits separately with switch "on."

LIGHTING SWITCH
Poor Contacts (Light Dim or Flicker)

1—Switch spider weak or loose.
2—Contacts dirty or corroded.

Switch Does Not Control Lights Properly

1—Improperly assembled. Spiders interfere with each other.

Lights Bright All Positions

1—Dimmer resistance shorted.
2—Resistance wire pressed together.
3—Insulation burned.

No Lights in Dim Position

1—Short or ground in lighting circuit.
2—Bulbs of higher voltage than resistance is designed to carry.

Lamps Do Not Light

1—Loose or broken connections between battery and switch.
2—Switch contacts weak and fail to make contact.

No Current Through Switch

1—Contacts on current limit relay held open.
2—Internal switch connections open.

Switch Grounded (Grounded System)

1—Damaged or defective insulation.
2—Terminal or cable touches switch case.
3—Short-circuit in wiring.

Open Circuit

1—Broken terminals.
2—No current from battery.

Switch Sticks (Plunger Type)

1—Plunger spring broken.
2—Plunger bent.
3—Terminal or movable contacts loose.

Switch Sticks (Handle Type)

1—Not lubricated.
2—Ratchet plate loose.
3—Excessive spring tension on ratchet.

SIGNAL LAMP SWITCH

Lamp Fails to Light

1—Defective switch.
2—Switch not actuated properly. Operating linkage not properly adjusted
to close switch as brakes are applied.
3—Hydraulic brake system. Switch defective or no fluid in brake system.
Brakes will not hold.

STARTING MOTOR

Motor Will Not Crank Enging

1—Battery weak or discharged.
2—Battery frozen.
3—Battery terminals loose, corroded, or broken.
4—Short-circuit in battery cable.
5—Starting switch open. No current from battery.
6—Foot switch does not depress fully.
7—Switch contacts burned.
8—Defective ignition switch. Starter and ignition switch in series.
9—Switch to motor wire insulation broken.
10—Motor brushes worn or broken.
11—Motor brush lead broken.
12—Motor brushes sticking in holders.
13—Motor brush ring grounded. Motor draws excessive current.
14—Poor seating brushes.
15—Upper brush does not make contact (motor-generator).
16—Generator brushes do not lift (motor-generator).
17—Motor commutator dirty.
18—Lead or terminal broken.
19—Armature grounded.
20—Armature shorted.
21—Open-circuited armature.
22—Armature rubs on pole piece.
23—Armature drags due to worn bearings.
24—Armature bearings tight or seized.
25—Field circuit open. No current drawn from battery.
26—Damaged Bendix drive pinion.
27—Bendix spring cap screw broken.
28—Gear teeth broken. Gear reduction motor.
29—Overrunning clutch rollers or springs broken.
30—Overrunning clutch worn.
31—Overrunning clutch tight on shaft due to lack of lubrication.
32—Bendix drive spring broken.
33—With Electric-Hand circuit breaker connected to clutch pedal, does not permit completion of starter circuit when clutch pedal is depressed.
34—Poor ground between engine and chassis.
35—*See also* Coincidental Starter.

Motor Cranks Engine Slowly

1—Battery weak.
2—Polarity of battery cells reversed.
3—Poor battery ground connection.
4—Starting switch grounded.
5—Poorly seated motor brushes.

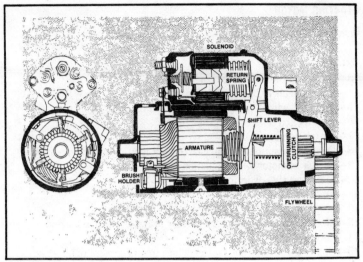

Starting motor.

6—Commutator dirty.
7—Weak brush springs.
8—Brush holder sticking (arcing at brushes).
9—Brush ring grounded.
10—Field windings shorted.
11—Grounded field coil.
12—*See also* Motor will not Crank Engine.

Starting Motor Turns; Engine Does Not Turn

1—Flywheel teeth broken.
2—Bendix drive pinion sticking on sleeve.
3—Bendix drive spring broken.
4—Bendix drive spring cap screw broken.
5—Bendix retarder pin spring too strong.
6—Bendix retarder pin bent or rusty.
7—Broken gears. Gear reduction motor.
8—Worn overrunning clutch does not engage.
9—Overrunning clutch center worn.
10—Overrunning clutch springs weak or broken.
11—Starter Startix adjusting screw in too far.
12—Improper connections at Startix.
13—Dirty or loose connections at Startix.

Starting Motor Runs at High Speed; Cranks Engine Slowly

1—Shorted field coils.
2—Grounded field coils.

Interrupted Cranking Intervals

1—Starter Startix adjusting screw out too far.

Starting Motor Spins with Engine

1—Bendix drive pinion sticking on sleeve.
2—Bendix drive spring broken.
3—Overrunning clutch center worn.
4—Overrunning clutch springs weak or broken.
5—Binding manual shift mechanism.
6—Switch button sticks.
7—Switch contacts burned.

Excessive Current Drawn by Motor

1—Lead or terminal broken.
2—Starting switch grounded.
3—Brush ring grounded.

Clicking Noise in Starter Gears

1—Generator not charging causing gears to clash.
2—Idling speed too low.

Starting Motor Noisy

1—Eccentric commutator.
2—Brushes noisy.
3—Starting motor out of alignment.
4—Pinion sticks in flywheel with car in motion due to worn retarder pin or weak spring.
5—Bendix drive gears improperly adjusted.
6—Damaged Bendix drive pinion.
7—Gear teeth broken (gear reduction motor).
8—Starter gears worn or battered.
9—Bearings worn or broken.
10—Worn bearings permitting excessive end play in armature.
11—Bearings seized to shaft.
12—Pole shoe loose.
13—Armature laminations damaged. Armature might be shorted.
14—Loose pilot screw on Bendix drive permitting motor to become loose in flywheel housing.
15—Overrunning clutch sticks. Pinion remains in mesh.

Starting Motor Rotation Reversed

1—Polarity reversed by wrong assembly of brush holder.
2—Wrong type of end housing.
3—Fields reversed.
4—Wrong fields assembled to motor.
5—Armature wound for different rotation.

Low Ammeter Reading Motor Running Idle

1—Low battery voltage at starter.
2—Poor brush contact on commutator.

High Ammeter Reading Motor Running Idle

1—Dirty or shorted armature.
2—Bent armature shaft.
3—Tight armature bearings.

Starting Motor Does Not Stop with Switch Released

1—Switch sticks.
2—Movable switch contact loose.
3—Plunger spring broken.
4—Plunger bent.
5—Terminals loose.

Poor Commutation

1—Imperfect brush contact.
2—Eccentric commutator.
3—Brush spring weak.
4—Brushes of wrong type or material.
5—Brush ring not properly adjusted.
6—Brush ring locking screws loose.
7—Dirty or greasy commutator.
8—High mica on commutator.
9—Open-circuited armature. Commutator is burned as bars are connected to open-circuited coils.

Commutator Burned

1—Weak brush spring tension.
2—Brush or holder sticks (arcing at brushes).
3—High mica on commutator.
4—Two-pole motors. Improper brush setting.

Rapid Brush Wear

1—Imperfect brush contact.
2—Eccentric commutator.
3—Excessive brush spring tension.
4—Commutator mica has been undercut. Turn down commutator.

Armature Throws Windings

1—Armature rubs on pole piece.
2—Loose pole shoe.
3—Worn armature bearings.

4—Bent or sprung armature shaft.
5—Failure of starter drive to release.

Armature Shorted

1—Defective insualtion.

Armature Open Circuited

1—Loose connections. Unsoldered at commutator.

Armature Rubs on Pole

1—Loose pole shoe.
2—Worn armature bearings.
3—Bent or sprung armature shaft.
4—Thrown windings due to failure of starter drive to release.

Heavy Sparking and Burning when Switch Is Depressed

1—Switch of motor wire loose or insulation broken.
2—Switch contacts make poor connection.

Switch Sticks

1—Spring broken.
2—Contact points burned.
3—Button sticks in switch body.

Starting Switch Grounded

1—Engine cranked slowly. Excessive current drawn from battery.

Starting Switch Open

1—Starting motor will not operate. No current drawn from battery.

Whirring Sound in Starter Drive

1—Broken Bendix drive spring.

Jingling Sound in Starter Drive.

1—Bendix counterweight loose on pinion.

Grating Noise in Starter Drive

1—Pinion contacting flywheel teeth. Bendix retarder pin spring weak.

Flywheel Teeth Broken

1—Starting motor out of alignment.
2—Spark advanced too far.
3—Preignition.

4—Ignition advance mechanism stuck.
5—Bendix drive spring weak.
6—Bendix pinion sticking.
7—Bendix sleeve sticking on armature shaft.
8—Armature shaft sprung.

Bendix Pinion Does Not Mesh with Flywheel

1—Starting motor out of alignment.
2—Bendix spring damaged.
3—Bendix spring cap screw broken.

Bendix Pinion Jams to Lock Engine

1—Excessive lubrication of Bendix drive.
2—Battery low. Not sufficient current for cranking operation.
3—Loose or broken pilot mounting screw.

Sluggish Disengagement of Starter Gears

1—Particularly in cold weather, weak return spring.

REMOTE STARTER CONTROL

Semiautomatic Starting.

Starter Fails to Operate

1—Defective switch.
2—Faulty push button switch.
3—Loose or dirty connections.
4—Defective wire or connection between push button and relay.
5—Faulty relay coil.
6—Unsoldered connections on solenoid lead wires.
7—Defective vacuum switch. Leaky diaphragm.

Starter Attempts to Engage with Engine Running

1—Idling speed too low. Should be high enough to keep ammeter indicating on "charge" side.
2—Defective push button switch.
3—Defective switch terminals.
4—Push-button switch bracket bent closing circuit.
5—Push-button binding in its mounting.
6—Switch binding due to bracket misalignment.
7—Weak or broken push button return spring.
8—With generator charging, ground in wire from switch to relay.
9—Connection between solenoid relay and generator ground terminal grounded.
10—Weak or broken hinge spring on solenoid relay armature.
11—With engine warm or high cranking speed, relay cutout voltage too low.

Starter Gears Do Not Engage

1—Broken or weak solenoid plunger return spring with relay contacts open.
2—Solenoid plunger dirty.
3—Solenoid relay does not close. Open circuit between starter button and ground, between starter button and relay, or through generator ground.
4—Improper calibration of relay or damaged windings.

Starter Revolves; Pinion Will Not Engage

1—Gummy clutch and pinion shaft.
2—Sticking solenoid plunger.

Sluggish Disengagement of Starter Gears

1—Weak torsional return spring tension at shift lever pivot.
2—Weak return spring in solenoid switch (particularly in cold weather if shaft is gummed up).

Starter Gears Do Not Disengage

1—Engine vacuum at full throttle not sufficient to operate accelerator switch.
2—Dirty solenoid plunger.
3—Solenoid relay contacts do not open.
4—Starter switch pull rod stuck.

Starter Switch Fails to Break Contact; Pinion Disengages

1—Starter switch rod sticks. Replace solenoid assembly.

Solenoid Starter Switch

1—Contacts dirty or pitted.
2—Terminals corroded or loose.
3—Generator not charging.
4—Improper adjustment of stud linkage.

Vacuum Switch

1—Leaky connections.
2—Defective switch.
3—Leaky diaphragm.
4—Loose mounting bolts.
5—Improper adjustment between accelerator pedal and switch or control mechanism.

Click Heard in Solenoid but Starter Does Not Operate

1—Dirty switch contacts.

2—Poor contact at starter brushes.

3—Short-circuited or open-circuited winding.

Click Not Heard in Solenoid

1—Linkage or control defective.

2—Accelerator rod binds.

3—Throttle return spring broken, disengaged, or out of adjustment.

4—Open-circuit prevents closing of solenoid relay.

Chevrolet Starterator

1—Starter control forks lack clearance under floorboard (⅛" clearance necessary).

2—Starter control link not at right angles to cross shaft.

3—Lack of clearance between face of starter control fork and accelerator rod (⅛" clearance necessary).

4—Lack of clearance between starter switch and starter link (5/16" clearance necessary).

COINCIDENTAL STARTER AND THROTTLE OPERATION

Starter Motor Does Not Crank
Engine with Accelerator Pedal Depressed

1—Accelerator does not return completely. This prevents the switch clutch from engaging.

2—Open circuit preventing closing of solenoid relay.

3—Improperly timed switch.

4—Solenoid contacts dirty.

5—Defective solenoid relay ground circuit.

6—Defective solenoid magnet coil.

7—Accelerator rod binds on floor mat.

8—Low battery.

9—Incomplete circuit.

STARTIX SWITCH

Prolonged Spinning of Starting Motor

1—Speed up engine to increase charging rate of generator.

2—Startix adjusting screw in too far.

Interrupted Cranking Intervals

1—Startix adjusting screw out too far.

Starter Turns, but Engine Does Not

1—Improper connections at Startix switch.

Clicking Sound

1—Pinion striking flywheel gear due to generator not charging. Temporarily remove small wire in ignition terminals at Startix and tape to insulate bare end.

2—Idling speed too low.

Battery Too Low to Crank Engine

1—Remove small wire at ignition terminal on Startix switch and tape to insulate the end. This will prevent pinion meshing when you are hand cranking. Pushing or towing is necessary to start the engine.

Startix Suspected of Being Defective

1—Make sure starting motor, generator, relay, and battery are in operating condition.

STARTING SWITCH

No Current through Switch (Starter Does Not Function)

1—Contacts burned.
2—Contacts broken.
3—Loose connections.

Switch Sticks (Release of Switch Does Not Stop Motor)

1—Plunger spring broken.
2—Plunger bent.
3—Terminals or movable contact loose.

Switch Grounded (Slow Cranking or Failure to Crank)

1—Damaged or defective insulation.
2—Terminal cable touches switch case.

No Current from Battery (Open Circuit)

1—Broken terminals.
2—Insulating material between contacts.

WIRING

Heavy Sparking and Burning

1—Short circuit.

Wiring Hot

1—Wires not properly connected.
2—Insulation broken.
3—Grounded circuit.

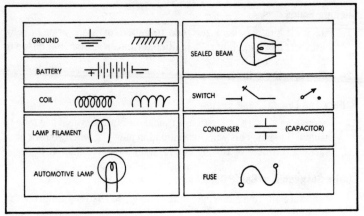

Wiring symbols.

Insulation Burned

1—Short circuit.
2—Grounded circuit.

Fuse Burned Out

1—Short circuit.
2—Broken or loose wire connections.
3—Insulation damaged.
4—Wires grounded to frame.

Battery Gradually Discharges

1—Chafed insulation on wires.
2—Leaks through armed cable around leads.
3—Top of battery wet.

No Discharge Reading at Ammeter (Switch "On")

1—Broken or loose connections.
2—Corroded terminals.

Ground or Short

1—Bare wire or terminal in contact with metal part.
2—Damaged or defective insulation.

Open Circuit

1—Broken wire or connection.
2—Loose screw or nut breaking contact at terminal.
3—Terminals unsoldered.
4—Blown fuse.

Loose Connection

1—Broken wire.
2—Loose screw or nut on terminal.
3—Connection unsoldered.

High Resistance

1—Loose or corroded connections.
2—Wires partly broken.
3—Wires too small for current carried in circuit.
4—Fuse loose in mounting.
5—Switch contacts burned or corroded.

WARNING SIGNALS

Note: Unless otherwise stated, analysis applies to both vibrator and motor-driven horns. (M) applies to motor-driven horns only; (V) applies to vibrator-type horns only.

Horn Inoperative

1—Blown fuse.
2—Low or discharged battery. No battery voltage applied to horn.
3—Horn button does not make contact (frequent source of trouble). Pushing button should show ammeter deflection.
4—Wire from battery to horn or horn to horn button broken or grounded.
5—Horn button not grounded where ground is necessary.
6—Loose wire connections at battery, horn button, splices, or horn terminals.
7—Horn projector loose or cracked (usually along seam).
8—Open, shorted, or burned-out field coil in horn.
9—Broken or unsoldered held coil lead.
10—(V) Broken, burned, pitted or improperly adjusted contact points.
11—(V) Broken or warped contact spring.
12—(V) Contact broken off at contact spring.
13—(V) Loose horn cover screws.
14—(M) No contact between brushes and commutator.

Horn Functions Only at Times

1—Poor contacts in horn button.
2—Loose or corroded connections.
3—(M) Shorted armature.
4—(M) Dirty commutator.

Horn Tone Not Standard after Adjustment

1—Incorrect armature air gap.
2—Incorrect voltage draw. It is important that both voltage and current be correct when measured at the horn.

3—Loose electrical connections.
4—Loose armature.
5—Loose circuit breaker screws.
6—Bad condenser.
7—Loose resonator disc.
8—Broken diaphragm.
9—Broken or loose projector.
10—Loose horn bracket.
11—Improper mounting.
12—On all Auto-Lite HC and HF horns, air leaks around the air column.
13—On all Auto-Lite HC and HF horns, armature striking core—producing
    a metallic sound.

Loss of Tone Quality

1—Worn or corroded contacts at horn button.
2—Low battery.
3—Voltage drop resulting from use of undersize wire.
4—Excessive voltage due to faulty generator condition.
5—Loose horn bracket screws.
6—Horn out of adjustment.
7—Improper current adjustment.
8—(V) Broken armature spring.
9—(V) Defective condenser.
10—(V) Incorrect air gap.
11—(M) Poor brush contact.
12—(M) Lack of lubrication.
13—(M) Two or more commutator bars shorted to each other.
14—(M) Armature wire unsoldered, broken, or shorted to armature lamina-
    tions.
15—*See also* Horn Inoperative.

Noisy Tone

1—Incorrect mounting.
2—Loose connections.
3—Diaphragm cracked.

Rough, Scratchy Tone

1—Loose terminals or connections.
2—(V) Pitted contact points.
3—(V) Armature gap not spaced same distance at each end.
4—(M) High tooth on actuator.
5—(M) Actuator not properly assembled.

Low Tone

1—(V) Armature gap space too large.

High Tone

1—(V) Armature gap space too small

Uneven Flat Tone

1—Broken diaphragm.

Sputtering Sound

1—(V) Horn improperly adjusted. Current consumption too high.

Tinny or Flat Tone

1—(M) No gasket between motor and projector.

Burned Out Field Coils

1—Horn operated on battery of higher voltage than for which it was designed.
2—(M) Field coil wire shorted to motor yoke assembly.
3—(M) Defective insulation between terminal screw and rear bracket or between brush holder screw and motor yoke.

Excessive Arcing at Brushes (M)

1—Concave surface of brush does not fit commutator.
2—Dirty commutator.
3—One brush holder off center with respect to other brush holder.

Excessive Arcing at Contacts (V)

1—Horn not properly adjusted.
2—Broken armature spring.
3—Defective condenser.

Contacts Pitted and Burned (V)

1—Contacts not properly adjusted.

Loose Brushes (M)

1—Burned brush springs due to improper contact between brush and holder.

Loose Brush Holder (M)

1—Loose brush holder screw.

Armature Revolves but Horn Produces No Sound Except Squeal (M)

1—Horn out of adjustment.
2—Loose actuator.
3—Broken diaphragm.

Armature Does Not Revolve (M)

1—Horn out of adjustment.
2—Open field coil due to unsoldered or broken wire.

Armature Burned Out (M)

1—Lack of lubrication.
2—Horn out of adjustment.
3—Horn operated on higher voltage than for which it was designed.
4—Two or more commutator segments shorted to each other.

RADIO EQUIPMENT

Due to the variety of constructions employed and the various installation methods, the best practice in diagnosing radio trouble is to follow the maker's instructions, check carefully the installation of the set, and use suppressors at all points specified. The ignition system sets up most interference noise and this is also the easiest to identify. As ignition takes place at consistent intervals, the rhythm of the noise will be very steady. Generator interference causes a "whirring buzz." Although there are many sources of interference and conditions that can affect the performance of the set, the following will prove of assistance in tracing trouble.

Set Does Not Operate

1—Defective tubes.
2—Batteries run down.
3—Antenna grounded or disconnected.
4—Set not grounded.
5—Defective switch.
6—Open circuit.
7—Set polarity reversed.

Weak Reception

1—Weak batteries.
2—Defective tubes.
3—High resistance in antenna.
4—Incorrect voltages.
5—Set oscillates.
6—Open antenna circuit.

Distorted Reception

1—Defective tubes.
2—Defective speaker.
3—Set oscillates.
4—Improper tuning.
5—Incorrect battery voltage.

Set Oscillates

1—Poor ground.
2—Defective condensers.
3—Broken or unsoldered connections.
4—Poor shielding.
5—Voltage too high.
6—Defective tube.
7—Out-of-alignment.

Poor Selectivity

1—Out-of-alignment.
2—Improper battery voltages.
3—Defective tubes.
4—Antenna too long or too short.

Tubes Do Not Light

1—Loose fuse.
2—Open fuses.
3—Defective tubes.
4—Open circuit between switch and set.
5—Poor contact at tubes.
6—Set not properly grounded.

Short Tube Life

1—Excessive voltage.
2—High generator charging rate.
3—Poor connections in car wiring.
4—Inferior tubes.
5—Improper adjustment of voltage regulator.

Intermittent Signals

1—Defective tubes.
2—Broken antenna lead-in.
3—Loose battery connections.
4—Open soldered joints.

Ignition: High-Tension Circuit Interference

1—Defective ignition coil. Break in secondary.
2—Defective insulation on high tension wires.
3—Burned or pitted breaker points.
4—Breaker points not properly adjusted.
5—Defective condenser in ignition system.
6—Excessive gap between distributor rotor and contact segments in cap.
7—Poor distributor ground. Ground distributor to motor block with flexible ground wire.

8—Ignition coil too close to radio.
9—High tension leaks in distributor cap.
10—Low and high-tension wires in same shield or manifold.
11—Spark plug gaps too wide.
12—Spark plug suppressors defective.
13—Distributor suppressor defective.
14—Suppressors have too low resistance value.

Ignition: Low-Tension Circuit Interference

1—Improperly grounded set.
2—Improperly grounded battery boxes.
3—Improperly grounded speaker cable.
4—Improperly grounded antenna lead-in wire shielding.
5—Improperly shielded dome light wire.

Generator Interference

1—Arcing of brushes.
2—Armature core clips pole piece.
3—Dirty commutator.
4—Defective cutout.
5—Defective brush holders.
6—Defective field connections.

General Interference

1—High resistance between radio set and antenna.
2—Antenna lead-in broken at antenna.
3—Battery terminals corroded.
4—Loose connections in one or more of the electrical circuits.

Static Interference

1—Dry fan belt. Work with mixture of glycerine and water to soften.
2—Passenger or driver picks up motor noise at floor board and transmitting this through his or her body to the antenna in car. Place copper screen wire under floor board.
3—Imitation leather upholstery or seat covers generating static by friction with passengers' clothing. Use cotton seat covers.
4—Brakes dragging.

Wheel Static Interference

1—Noise almost a continuous roar.

Vibrator Points Fused Together

1—Starting engine with radio turned on.
2—Overcharged battery.
3—High voltage.

BRAKES

When making an analysis of brake troubles, keep in mind that any brake system will not function normally immediately following the washing of the car until the brakes have been applied a few times. This ungovernable condition is caused by moisture on the brake linings. Alterations in adjustment are not necessary. The absolute futility of attempting to make accurate brake adjustments with wet linings should be carefully considered. The brake linkage is generally set to standard specifications. Before attempting adjustments, always consult a brake chart for the particular vehicle. Also make sure that the linkage operates freely and that all levers will return to their respective stops with the brakes in the "off" or released

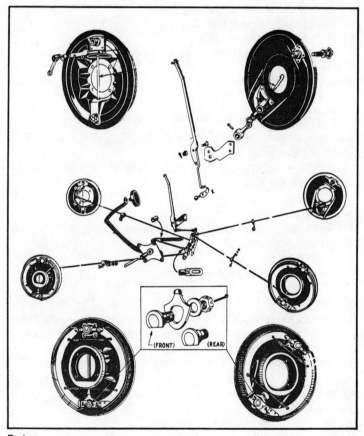

Brakes.

position. Adjustment for lining wear or for equalization must always be made at the shoes.

General Brake Troubles

Brakes Not Holding

1—Unequal or improper adjustment.
2—High spots on linings.
3—Dust, sand, rust, or foreign matter on linings.
4—Glazed or hard lining.
5—Loose rivets.
6—Lining worn (rivets touching drum).
7—Grease on lining or drum.
8—Bands or shoes out of shape.
9—Drums expanding.
10—Eccentric or scored drums.
11—Ends of shoes or band touching drum.
12—Rusted or dry moving parts.
13—Worn or twisted anchor pins.
14—Release spring too strong.
15—Loose rods.
16—Too much adjustment on pull rods.
17—Lever positions incorrect.
18—Equalizer off center.
19—Linkage binding.
20—Loose wheel bearings, drums, or shields.
21—Shoe guides loose (GMC brakes).

One Brake Will Not Hold

1—Lining worn.
2—Flared brake drum.
3—Bent brake parts interfering with operation.
4—Grease on lining.
5—Linkage not moving freely.
6—Refer also to brakes not holding.

Unbalanced Brakes

1—Too much variation in brake lining clearance at opposite ends of shoe. A combination of adjustments that increases action on some shoes and decreases it on others will unbalance brakes.
2—Distorted brake shoes or loose lining on one or more shoes.

Brakes Fade on Hills

1—Drums expanding.
2—Shoes require adjustment for clearance.
3—Shoes fitted with very poor linings.

Brakes Fade Under All Conditions

1—Grease from wheel bearings running out onto brake lining.
2—Wrong type of grease used.
3—*See also* Brakes Fade on Hills.

Car Pulls to One Side

1—Too tight a brake adjustment on any one front wheel.
2—One or more brakes grab.
3—Sticky or gummed lining; grease-soaked lining.
4—Loose lining. Loose rivets.
5—Clearance adjustment worn or lost.
6—Shoes or bands twisted out of shape.
7—Drums scored or out-of-round.
8—Dust shield loose.
9—Rusted brake linkage.
10—Equalizer rusted off center.
11—Loose front spring U-bolts.
12—Weak or sagged front springs.
13—Misalignment of front springs.
14—Tires not properly inflated.
15—Excessive play in steering linkage.
16—Loose wheel bearings.
17—Adjustment on kick shackle side too tight.
18—Condition of tire tread. Smooth tread will lock readily.
19—*See also* Brakes Grab.

Brakes Grab

1—Lack of linkage lubrication.
2—Grease or brake dope on lining.
3—Wet or sticky lining.
4—Nonuniform lining.
5—Loose lining. Loose rivets.
6—Anchor clearance too great.
7—Retractor springs unseated or improperly located.
8—Drums out-of-round.
9—Badly worn shoes, band support, or hinge pins.
10—Improper adjustment.
11—Loose, worn, or twisted anchor pins.
12—Too much self-energizing action.
13—Equalizer frozen off center.
14—Insecure anchorage of cable conduit.
15—Loose wheel bearings.
16—Loose spring U-bolts.
17—Weak chassis springs. Axle roll.
18—Loose pivot bearings. Knee action suspension.
19—*See also* Brakes Chatter.

Failure to Release

1—Axle roll or axle shifting on springs.
2—Frozen bearings in brake linkage.
3—Weak retractor springs.
4—Linkage not adjusted to stops.
5—*See also* Brakes Drag.

Brakes Drag

1—High spots on lining.
2—Shoes or bands out of true.
3—Rusty brake mechanism.
4—Ends of shoes or bands touching drum.
5—Drums scored or out-of-round.
6—Improper or unequal clearance adjustment. Adjusted while hot.
7—Improper leverage or obstruction.
8—Broken or weak retractor springs.
9—Retractor springs unseated or improperly located.
10—Interference between pedal and floor board or linkage and chassis.
11—Loose king pins or wheel bearings.
12—Loose pivot bearings. Knee action suspension.
13—Worn backing plate. Hard pedal.

Brakes Chatter

1—Improper adjustment.
2—Excessive anchor clearance.
3—Anchor pins twisted, loose, or worn.
4—Grease or dope on lining.
5—Lining loose on rivets.
6—Badly worn brake shoe, band support, or hinge pins.
7—Weak or loose backing plate.
8—Worn pins in brake lining.
9—Dry or rusty control linkage parts.
10—Rod movement obstructed.
11—Cable improperly adjusted.
12—Drums out-of-round or scored.
13—Drums loose on wheel hub.
14—Loose wheel bearings.
15—Broken or weak retractor springs.
16—Retractor springs lost or detached.
17—Axle loose on spring seats.
18—Loose spring U-bolts.
19—Weak chassis springs.
20—External bands. Band adjustment too loose.

Noisy Brakes

1—Brake pedal rubbing on toe board.

Brakes Chatter when Making Turn

1—Short cable conduits.

Brakes Squeal or Squeak

1—Brakes dragging.
2—Localized high pressure due to uneven adjustment.
3—Glazed or grease soaked linings.
4—Gravel, dust, or foreign matter between lining and drum.
5—Drum rust or metallic rust on lining.
6—Metallic particles worn from drum imbedded in lining.
7—New lining contacting ridge worn in drum.
8—Harmonic vibration of drums due to loose parts or rivets touching drum.
9—Loose, worn, or twisted anchor stud or backing plate.
10—Distorted brake shoe or band.
11—Frozen anchor pins or cams.
12—Thin drums distorted under pressure.
13—Scored or eccentric drums.
14—Frozen equalizer.
15—Loose rods or linkage causing vibration.
16—Loose wheel bearings.
17—Brake shoe guides loose (GMC brakes).
18—Bulge at rivet holes not removed.
19—Too much clearance at anchor end of shoes.

Brakes Rattle

1—Incorrect adjustment.
2—Broken or weak retractor springs.
3—Broken or weak anti-rattle springs.
4—Weak brake shoe guides (GMC brakes).

Springy Brakes

1—Improper truing of drums.
2—Weak drums. Distorting under brake pressure.
3—Linkage stretching.
4—Cross shafts and brake shafts twisting.
5—Levers bending.

Erratic Brake Action

1—Broken front spring leaf clips.

Brakes Apply Themselves in Reverse

1—Front brake linkage adjusted too tightly. Linkage does not compensate for play in knuckle bushings and tipping of front axle.

Sluggish Pedal

1—Lack of linkage lubrication.
2—Weak retractor springs in brakes or on linkage.

Drums Scoring

1—Soft drums.
2—Lining picking up metal from surface due to soft drums.
3—Protruding rivet heads.
4—Lining unsuited to requirements.
5—Attempting to get maximum contact of lining by "burning in." This is especially true with hard or dense lining.
6—Linings worn.
7—Localized pressure due to maladjustment or eccentric drum.

Drum Distortion

1—Drums too thin or weak.
2—Drums turned with thin wall.
3—Unequal pressure on hub bolts or mounting.

Drums Heat Excessively

1—Loose wheel bearings.
2—Drums eccentric-out-of-round.
3—Shoes binding on backing plates.
4—Weak return springs permitting brakes to drag.

Cracked or Heat Checked Brake Drums

1—Drums eccentric (resulting in localized pressure and overheating).
2—Brakes dragging.
3—Unnecessary abrupt braking by operator.
4—Abrupt cooling of heated drum by running through water.

Swelling and Binding

1—Too tight or improper adjustment.
2—Dope on brake lining.
3—Dragging at one point causing drum to expand.

Uneven Lining Wear

1—Clearance between lining and drum too small.
2—High spots on lining.
3—Weak retractor springs.
4—Rough drums.
5—Eccentric or scored drums.

Lining Wears Rapidly

1—Brakes dragging.

2—Unequal adjustment.
3—Too little clearance between lining and drum.
4—Lining too soft or too hard or scored drums.
5—Rough drums.
6—Play in spring shackles, bolts, etc.
7—Play in steering parts.
8—Improper front wheel toe-in.
9—*See also* Uneven Lining Wear.

Lining Glazed

1—Coated with grease and dust.
2—Coated with drum rust.
3—Coated with particles of drum steel and rivets.

Grease Appears on Brake Linings

1—Wrong type of grease used for wheel bearings.
2—Wheel bearing over lubricated.
3—Pressure gun used in lubrication bearings causing overlubrication also forces grease into brake drum.

Brakes Lock when Backing

1—Brake shoes not properly centered.
2—Brake linkage shortened too much.

Brakes Lock when Cold and Slip when Hot

1—Grease on lining.

One Wheel Locks when Car Hits Bump

1—Broken rear spring.
2—Loose spring U-bolts.

Wheel Locks at Same Point Every Time

1—Eccentric brake drum.
2—Lining coated with grease.

One Brake Drags

1—Shoe return springs on opposite brakes do not have uniform tension.

Wheel Locks when Hot or Cold

1—Improper anchor adjustment.
2—Weak brake return springs.
3—Frozen linkage or cross-shaft bearings.
4—Excessive play in spring shackles.
5—Loose spring U-bolts.
6—Sheared spring center bolt.

Lining Burns After Adjustment

1—Burns at top with external brake or bottom with internal brakes. Wheel bearings out of adjustment.

Popping Noise when Applied

1—Drum grooved or threaded. Shoes being pulled away from backing plate and then snapping back.

2—Bendix: wrong assembly of shoe return springs.

Poor Equalization

1—Drums on opposite wheels not of same thickness.

2—Unequal mechanical advantage due to wrong adjustment of levers and linkage.

Brakes Effective (Drums Cold) and Ineffective (Drums Hot)

1—Grease on linings.

Note: Grease on lining is frequently mentioned as a source of trouble. This in general is brought about by the use of power lubrication to lubricate the wheel bearings and brake assembly inside the brake drum. To avoid this condition, hand lubrication should be employed.

Bendix Brakes

Brakes Not Holding

1—Anchor pins shifted.
2—Lever positions incorrect.
3—Too much adjustment on rods or linkage.
4—Linings worn.
5—Grease on lining.
6—Glazed lining.
7—Grit or metal dust on lining.
8—Drum rust on lining.
9—Rivets touching drum.
10—Drums scored or out-of-round.

One Brake Does Not Hold

1—Grease on lining.
2—Rods and levers not moving freely.
3—Bent brake parts interfering with operation.

Brakes Grab

1—Anchor pins loose.
2—Loose brake camshaft brackets.
3—Lining coated with grease.
4—Loose lining.

5—Sticky lining.

6—Scored or out-of-round drums.

7—Equalizer rusted off center.

8—Loose wheel bearings.

9—Loose spring U-bolts.

10—Shoe return springs reversed. The heaviest spring must always be attached to the top shoe.

Brakes Drag

1—Broken or weak return springs.

2—Return springs detached or removed.

3—Return springs not properly assembled.

4—Rusty or dry brake linkage and control parts.

5—Pedal or rod movement restricted by body or chassis.

6—Improper adjustment, particularly at eccentric, adjusted while hot.

7—Loose dust shield or carrier bracket.

Brakes Chatter

1—Anchor pins not properly adjusted.

2—Unequal brakes.

3—Lining loose on rivets.

4—Grease soaked lining.

5—Drums scored or out-of-round.

6—Loose spring U-bolts.

7—Loose wheel bearings.

Brakes Squeak

1—Dust accumulation between lining and drum.

2—Exposed rivets touching drum.

3—Dirty or glazed lining.

4—Loose rivets.

5—Drums out-of-round.

6—Loose anchor pins.

7—Unequal brakes.

8—Rusty or dry moving parts of brake.

9—Loose wheel bearings or drums.

10—Bulge at rivet holes in lining causing high spots.

Noisy Brakes

1—Loud clicks. Shoe return springs reversed. Heaviest spring must always be attached to secondary shoe.

2—Popping noise. Edge of shoe hanging slightly on dust shield before centralizing. Smooth edge and lubricate slightly.

Brakes Rattle

1—Spring does not return shoes to proper position.

2—Guides worn or broken.

3—Resistance in linkage. Shoes do not fully release.
4—Brake rods and linkage loose.

Lining Wears Rapidly

1—Brakes dragging.
2—Drums scored.

Lining Glazed

1—Dirt on lining, etc.

Hard Pedal

1—Improper lining.

MIDLAND STEELDRAULIC BRAKES

No Pedal Reserve (Pedal Goes to Floorboard)

1—Reset anchor pin at 1/16" clearance.
2—Centralize brake shoe band in drum.
3—Adjust all brakes for equalization.

Hard Pedal

1—Brakes not equalized.
2—Too much pedal reserve. Pedal too high.
3—Binding in cross shaft.
4—Grease on lining.
5—Exceedingly poor lining to drum contact.
6—Lining coated with road dust.

Ineffective Brakes

1—Complete readjustment needed.
2—Improper lining on shoe (only lining specified by vehicle maker should
   be used).
3—Lining worn out.

Brakes Drag

1—Shoes not properly adjusted (adjusted while hot).
2—Shoe clearance too large.
3—Too much anchor pin clearance.
4—Lining not of proper thickness.
5—Damaged shoe.
6—Broken retractor springs.

Brakes Cannot Be Equalized

1—Anchor clearance not equal at all four brakes.

Frequent Adjustment Necessary

1—Use of other than recommended lining.
2—Improper adjustment.
3—Drums expanding.

Car Pulls to Left or Right

1—Brakes not properly adjusted.
2—Grease on lining.
3—Loose front-spring U-bolts.
4—Uneven tire pressure.
5—Different kinds of lining on the brakes or not the recommended type.

Brakes Squeal

1—High spots on lining surface.
2—Linings not chamfered properly.
3—Loose rivets.
4—Adjusters not fitting snugly on leg of shoe.
5—Lining not fitted tight to shoe.

Brakes Rattle

1—Shoe spread at toggle pivot pin point.
2—Cam bent away from rigid shoe.
3—Toggle loose due to loose cable.
4—Broken, bent, or weak anti-rattler.
5—Lack of clearance between anchor pin and adjuster.

Sluggish Pedal

1—Cable jammed in conduit.

Play in Pedal

1—Improper adjuster to anchor pin clearance.

Scored Drums

1—Foreign matter or steel from drums picked up by lining or rivets heads.

Eccentric Lining Wear

1—Shoe or band not properly located in drum.

Frozen Cable Conduits

1—Broken cable strand.
2—Lack of lubrication.

Short Cable Conduits

1—Chatter when making turn.

Adjustment

1—Take up slack in cables or rods to produce correct anchor pin clearance.
2—Centralize shoes in drum at centralizing cams.
3—Adjust brakes for equalization at adjusting nut.

LOCKHEED HYDRAULIC BRAKES

Wagner and Bendix types.

Pedal Goes to Floor Board

1—Normal wear of brake lining.
2—Brake Shoes not properly adjusted.
3—Low fluid level in reservoir.
4—Air in system.
5—Leaks in system.
6—Pedal improperly set.
7—Improper fluid in system. Vapor lock (fluid boiling) due to high temperature.
8—After dragging brakes, cool and rebleed system. Flush the system with alcohol if mineral oil has been used.

All Brakes Drag

1—Mineral oil, etc., in the system.
2—Dirt in master cylinder compensating port hole.
3—Pedal improperly set.
4—Brake shoe clearance too small (adjusted while hot).
5—Piston cups swollen through use of mineral oil.
6—Pedal does not return to stop.
7—Weak shoe return springs.
8—Vent hole in master cylinder filler cap clogged (retarding return of fluid from lines).

One Wheel Drags

1—Weak brake shoe return spring.
2—Brake shoe bearing seized to anchor pin.
3—Brake shoes set too close to drum.
4—Wheel cylinder piston cups distorted.
5—Grease on lining (mud, water, etc.) in brakes.
6—Wheel cylinder pistons or cups frozen in cylinder.
7—Loose wheel bearings.
8—Brake shoe eccentric. Not properly adjusted.
9—Obstruction in line.
10—Worn backing plate bushings on crank-arm suspension.

Brakes Tighten After Adjustment

1—Pedal stop screw loose. This causes short return of pedal to close master cylinder compensating port.

2—Swollen rubber cups in system.

Shoe Clearance Cannot Be Maintained Immediately after Adjustment

1—Adjusting cam loose on adjusting bolt.

Car Pulls to One Side

1—Grease-soaked lining or mud, water, etc., in brakes.

2—Shoes not properly adjusted.

3—Lining worn or drum scored.

4—Different makes of linings on shoes (not of specified type).

5—Tires not properly inflated or unequal wear of thread. Different tread nonskid design.

6—Front spring U-bolts loose.

7—Dust shield loose on axle.

8—Restriction (dent or kink) in lines.

9—Loose wheel bearings.

10—Worn backing plate bushings on crank-arm suspension.

11—Primary and secondary shoes reversed.

12—Both sets of front and rear shoes not relined at the same time.

Brakes Sluggish

1—Fluid not suited to atmospheric conditions. This is especially true in subzero temperatures.

2—All brake shoe retracting springs not of same tension (sluggish release).

One Wheel Locks

1—Obstruction in fluid line at wheel prevents return of fluid to lines.

Brakes Cannot Be Equalized

1—On cylinders of step-bore construction, cylinders not properly placed with reference to bore size.

2—Different makes of linings on shoes (not the same on all shoes).

3—Distorted brake shoes or loose lining on one or more shoes.

Loss of Pedal Pressure in Hot Weather

1—Inferior fluid boiling in system boiling (causing vapor lock).

Pedal Cannot Be Adjusted

1—Pedal stop lock ring out of seat in master cylinder.

Springy, Spongy Pedal

1—Brake shoes not properly adjusted.
2—Air in system.
3—Air introduced in rear wheel cylinders by use of parking brake.

Brake Pedal Jams

1—Use of nongenuine fluid in system.
2—Defective cylinder cups and washers.
3—Piston stop lock wire out of master cylinder groove.

Excessive Pressure on Pedal (Poor Stop)

1—Brake shoes not properly adjusted.
2—Improper brake lining.
3—Oil or grease on linings.
4—Lining making partial contact on drum.
5—Worn anchor pins.
6—Linings improperly installed.

Light Pressure on Pedal (Severe Brakes)

1—Brake shoes not properly adjusted.
2—Loose dust shield on axle.
3—Loose backing plate hub bushing crank-arm suspension.
4—Grease soaked or worn linings; scored drums.
5—Worn linings.
6—Scored drums.

Brakes Squeak

1—Improperly ground shoes. High spots on linings.
2—Backing plates bent or shoes twisted.
3—Metallic particles imbedded in linings.
4—Drums scored or out-of-round.
5—Too much clearance at anchor end of shoes.

Uneven Lining Wear

1—Defective wheel cylinder or cup.

All Air Cannot Be Bled from Lines

1—Defective wheel cylinder cup.
2—Master piston seal collapses to permit air to enter system from supply tank. Pressure bleeding will correct this trouble.
3—On old types with mechanically operated stoplight switch. Pedal travel on release excessive due to switch spring tension.
4—Air introduced in rear wheel cylinders by use of parking brake.

One Brake Cannot Be Bled

1—Pinched copper tubing at wheel cylinder closing line.
2—Rubber tubing clogged due to deterioration caused by use of inferior fluid.

Slow Returning Pedal

1—Rough master cylinder or wheel cylinders.
2—Hardened piston cup.
3—Rough cylinder and hardened piston cup.
4—Weak pedal return spring.
5—Pedal binding on its mounting.

One Brake Does Not Hold

1—Wrong type of fluid used causing disintegration of rubber hose and clogging of lead to wheel cylinder.
2—Flattened copper tube at axle connection shutting off pressure to wheel cylinder.
3—Frozen wheel cylinder pistons.

Brakes Grunt or Groan when Applying Pedal

1—Tight fitting master or wheel cylinder.
2—Piston cups assembled dry.
3—Dirty cylinders.

Loss of Fluid from System

1—Leakage in piping or fittings.
2—Defective filler gasket or baffle in master cylinder reservoir.
3—Defective piston cups.
4—Scored cylinder castings.

Leaky Wheel Cylinders

1—Too much shoe clearance permitting excessive travel of wheel cylinder cups and pistons.
2—Rough cylinder bore (grooved, pitted, or corroded).

FORD MECHANICAL BRAKES

See also General Brake Troubles

Brakes Will Not Hold

1—Wear in mechanism destroying lever position and alignment.

Brakes Drag

1—High spots on lining. Relined shoes not ground.
2—Brake shoes not concentric with drum (not centralized).

3—Insufficient lining clearance.
4—Adjustment made with brakes hot.
5—Worn adjusting screw or wedge.

One Wheel Drags

1—Loose nut on operating wedge at backing plate.

Car Pulls To One Side

1—Bent radius rod.
2—Unequal tire pressure.
3—Different linings used.
4—Grease or oil on linings.
5—Adjustment not maintained for each wheel individually.
6—Brake linkage binds.
7—Brake shoes distorted.

Brakes Chatter

1—Improperly adjusted brake rods.
2—Loose wheel bearing.
3—Loose steering knuckle pin bearings.
4—Brake housing plate loose on spindle or axle.
4—Improperly distributed clearance between lining and drum.
6—Oil-soaked lining.
7—Loose front axle connection or spring perches.
8—Lining not chamfered at ends.
9—Too much play in floating mounting of shoes.
10—Loose radius rods.
11—Lining of uneven thickness.

Brakes Squeak

1—Improper ground shoes. High spots on lining.
2—Improper adjustment.
3—Oil-soaked linings.

Hard Pedal

1—Wear permits operating lever to pull past vertical center.

Drum Distortion

1—Drums turned with thin wall.
2—Unequal pressure at hub bolts.

Clicking Noise

1—Loose wheel mounting at hub bolts.

Brakes Groan when Stopping

1—Shoes not rounded to drums.

STEWARD-WARNER POWER-OPERATED BRAKES

(*See also* General Brake Troubles)

Soft Pedal

1—Worn friction members in power unit.

Brakes Drag

1—Power unit adjustment set too close.
2—Lubricant in transmission too heavy.
3—Improperly adjusted power unit.
4—Cables sag causing brakes to stick.
5—Sticking brake camshaft due to lack of lubrication (lubricate sparingly).
6—Weak brake return springs.

Brake Cables Vibrate or Sag

1—Supporting clips improperly placed or omitted.

VACUUM BOOSTER-OPERATED BRAKES

B-K Booster Cylinder.

Insufficient Brakes

1—Foot pedal strikes floor board.
2—Grease or oil on linings.
3—Linings worn out.
4—Different brake linings.
5—Binding brake cross-shaft bearings.
6—New metal linings not worn-in.
7—Leaks in intake manifold.
8—Check valve connections reversed.
9—Faulty assembly.

Application Too Slow

1—Air cleaner obstructed.
2—Booster cylinder not lubricated.
3—Not enough vacuum.
4—Faulty assembly.

Brakes Drag

1—Might be due to slow release. Release port in control valve obstructed or too small.
2—Booster valve leaking slightly.

Release Too Slow

1—Booster cylinder not lubricated.
2—Pedal retracting spring too weak.
3—Wrong pedal valve stop adjustment.

Brakes Too Powerful

1—External retracting springs too weak.
2—Different brake linings (not specified type).
3—Faulty installation.

Leaks

1—Destroy vacuum in booster cylinder.

AIR-OPERATED BRAKE SYSTEM

Brakes Produce Rough Stop

1—Wrong application of pressure. Apply heavy pressure at start of application and ease off as speed is reduced.

Slow Brake Application

1—Low brake line pressure.
2—Brake chamber push rod travel excessive.
3—Restriction in line.
4—Leaking brake chamber diaphragm.
5—Poor brake lining condition.
6—Leaking brake valve diaphragm.

Slow Brake Release

1—Brake valve lever not returning fully to stop.
2—Binding cam or camshaft.
3—Brake chamber push rod travel excessive.
4—Improper seating of valves in brake valve.

Improper Action of System

1—Improper adjustment.
2—Leaks in system.
3—Moisture allowed to accumulate in reservoir (carried over into system).
4—Excessive push rod travel at brake chambers.
5—Brake chamber diaphragm leaking.

Compressor Fails to Build up Pressure

1—Broken lines or connections.

2—Stuck exhaust valve.
3—Drive belt loose or broken.

Compressor Builds up Pressure Slowly

1—Clogged suction manifold air cleaner.
2—Loose connection between manifold and compressor.
3—Leakage in piping or other parts of system.
4—Discharge valves not seating properly.
5—Defective piston packing rings.
6—Drive belt slipping.
7—Leaking application or brake valve.
8—Leaking compressor.
9—Carbon in discharge line.

Brake Application Sluggish or Gauge Pressure Drops

1—Intake strainer in brake valve clogged with dirt.
2—Intake strainer in application. Release valve clogged with dirt.

Compressor Heats Excessively

1—Lack of oil in compressor crankcase.
2—Air passages clogged with burnt oil.
3—Worn or cut piston packing rings.
4—Discharge valves have insufficient lift.
5—Weak valve springs.

Excessive Reduction of Reservoir Pressure on Full Application

1—Excessive stroke of brake chamber pull rods.
2—Leakage in brake valve exhaust valve.
3—Leakage in line between brake valve and brake chambers.
4—Leakage in brake inlet valve (brakes released).
5—Leakage in brake valve exhaust valve (brakes released).

Quick Loss of Reservoir Pressure with Engine Stopped

1—Worn and leaking compressor discharge valves.
2—Tubing or connections leaking.
3—Leaking valves.
4—Leaking governor.

Compressor Not Unloading

1—Broken unloader diaphragm.
2—Too much clearance in unloader valves.
3—Governor not operating.
4—Restriction in line from governor to unloader.

Leaks

1—Leaking intake valve.
2—Leaking exhaust valve.
3—Leaking governor valves.
4—Leaking drain cock at reservoir.
5—Leaking fittings or connections.
6—Leaking pipes or castings under pressure.
7—Leaking safety valve in reservoir.
8—Dirt in quick-release valve.
9—Defective quick-release valve diaphragm.
10—Defective diaphragm in brake chambers.

Knock in Compressor

1—Worn connecting rod bearings.

Application Valve Squeals

1—Spring and diaphragm dry (coat with gear oil).

No Whistle on Release of Brakes

1—Intake strainer in brake valve clogged with dirt.
2—Intake strainer in application. Release valve clogged with dirt.

System Frozen

1—Moisture allowed to accumulate and freezes in system.

Damaged Storage Tank

1—Mounting strap loose allowing tank to vibrate.

WARNER ELECTRIC BRAKE

Erratic Action

1—Worn wheel bearings.
2—Loose wheels.

Brakes Lack Holding Ability

1—Undersized brakes.
2—Insufficient current (minimum requirement 3 amperes per brake).
3—Grease on linings.
4—Improper lining (moulded lining having coefficient of .4 required).
5—Worn drums (maximum allowable wear ⅛").
6—Improper spacing of magnets and armatures (armature must be pressed against magnet not less than ⅛" or more than 5/32").
7—Worn linings.

Brakes Lock

1—Bands out of round.
2—Drums out of round.
3—Improper lining.

Clutches, Chassis, Springs, and Things

CLUTCH

Clutch Slips

1—Too little free pedal travel. Clutch pedal riding floor board.
2—Driver allows foot to rest on clutch pedal.
3—Transmission out of alignment.
4—Worn clutch facings.
5—Clutch spring pressure insufficient either due to improper adjustment, weak springs, or friction faces are worn or oily.
6—Grease on clutch facings.
7—Bent or warped discs or plates.
8—Weak or broken clutch springs.
9—Improper adjustment of clutch release levers.
10—Distorted pressure plate.
11—Cushion tabs on driven disc bent in while refacing disc. Also results in poor engagement.
12—Driving pins or bolts in pressure plate binding.

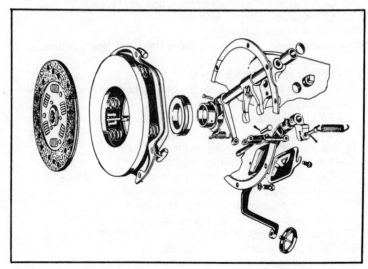

Clutch.

Clutch Grabs

1—Worn clutch facings.
2—Gummy clutch facings.
3—Bent or warped discs or plates. Binding or sticking parts.
4—Hard or dry facings.
5—Grease on clutch facings.
6—Improper adjustment of clutch that is provided with an adjustment for facing wear.
7—Misalignment of clutch bell housing.
8—Improper adjustment of clutch release levers.
9—Distorted pressure plate.
10—Bent clutch shaft.
11—Flywheel surface not smooth or clean (causing misalignment of clutch).
12—Facings damaged by rough flywheel surface.
13—Pressure plate binding on studs.
14—Bent cover throwing release levers out of adjustment.
15—Wrong type of facing used.
16—Clutch has been slipping and intense heat has distorted crimped driven plate.
17—Pedal sticking caused by shaft binding.

Clutch Drags (Spins when Released)

1—Too much free pedal travel (improper adjustment).
2—Driver does not release clutch fully.
3—Clutch improperly adjusted (adjustment too tight).
4—Clutch release bearing defective.
5—Grease on clutch facings.
6—Poor riveting. Clutch facing not held parallel, not held tight, or flat against driven disc.
7—Bent or warped clutch plates.
8—Discs or plates do not slide freely on splines or studs.
9—Gummy or sticky clutch facings.
10—Flywheel surface not smooth or clean (causing misalignment of clutch).
11—Facings damaged by rough flywheel surface.
12—Release levers not properly adjusted.
13—Bent cover throwing release levers out of alignment.
14—Pressure plate or center drive disc binding.
15—Pressure plate cracked, broken, or warped.
16—Pilot bearing worn or frozen on shaft.
17—Separator springs on center drive plate worn or broken.
18—Misalignment of clutch bell housing.
19—Cushion tabs on driven disc bent out while refacing disc.
20—Engine idling speed too high. Adjust throttle stop screw.

Clutch Pedal Pulsation or Vibration

1—Toggle levers unevenly adjusted.
2—Clutch housing sprung by improper installation.
3—Clutch release shaft arms not parallel.
4—Clutch release shaft bent.
5—Clutch pedal pull back spring missing or broken.
6—Severe case of misalignment between transmission and engine assembly.
7—Flywheel not properly seated on crankshaft flange.
8—Bent crankshaft or flywheel flange.

Clutch Chatter

1—Maladjustment of clutch disengaging mechanism.
2—Maladjustment of clutch release levers.
3—Grease on clutch facings. Dust in clutch.
4—Clutch facings worn or glazed.
5—Unequal clutch spring pressure. Release levers binding.
6—High spot on clutch pressure plate.
7—Facing dust on flywheel surface.
8—Cracked or broken pressure plate.
9—Insufficient cushion or dish in driven plate.
10—Warped or grooved pressure plate.
11—Flexible center or springs in driven member worn or broken.
12—Clutch shaft bent.
13—Lack of balance of pressure plate assembly.
14—Lack of balance of complete assembly.
15—Misalignment of clutch and transmission.
16—On clutch with disc universal joint inside plates, defective disc joint destroying balance of clutch shaft.
17—Universal joints on propeller shaft not in alignment.
18—Excessive end play in front shackles or rear springs.
19—Excessive backlash in universal joints or rear axle.
20—Pressure plate binding on pins or studs.
21—If the car is equipped with hill holder, this unit might not be properly adjusted.
22—Weak retractor springs (diaphragm spring type).

Clutch Noise

1—Throwout or pilot bearing need lubrication or worn out.
2—Transmission out of alignment causing clutch gear bushing to be misaligned with pilot bearing in flywheel.
3—Misapplication of clutch facing to plate.
4—Clutch parts binding.
5—Tips of release levers worn.
6—Splines in clutch hub worn.

7—Splines on clutch shaft worn.

8—Release levers dry or worn.

9—Broken release bolts.

10—Throwout bearing riding release lever.

11—Springs or rubber in flexible center of driven member worn or broken.

12—Vibration at clutch pedal. Clutch not centered in flywheel. Might result in noise similar to main bearing knock.

13—Centrifugal type: insufficient free pedal travel. Release levers contacting throwout bearing as they move back.

14—Grinding noise—worn release bearing.

15—Click or rattle: Release levers out of adjustment.

Buzz in Clutch

1—Clutch release spring unfastened.

Clutch Rattles

1—Excessive play between discs and driving studs.

2—Excessive play between hub and clutch shaft splines.

3—Clutch dowel pins worn.

4—Weak or broken clutch springs.

5—Clutch release bearing worn.

6—Lack of lubrication or worn pilot bearing.

7—Driving pins or bolts in pressure plate worn.

8—Torsional vibration of engine transmitted through clutch without vibration damper.

9—Clutch shaft or release sleeve out of line.

10—Noticeable at idling speeds, clutch levers riding at an uneven plane. The run-out should not exceed. 002″.

Clutch Release Bearing Noisy

1—Insufficient lubrication.

2—Dirt in bearing.

3—Worn or broken bearing.

4—Release member not in alignment with bearing.

5—Improper clutch pedal adjustment.

6—Misalignment of clutch and transmission.

Clutch Squeaks

1—Insufficent pedal to floorboard clearance.

2—Defective release bearing.

3—Clutch brake surface rough.

4—Release bearing or retainer not out of alignment.

5—Loose thrust washer on clutch shaft.

6—Bent clutch shaft.

7—Pilot bearing worn.

126

8—Lack of clearance between release levers and bearings.
9—Release parts not lubricated.
10—Misalignment between engine, clutch, and transmission.

Vibration

1—Use of rigid clutch plate where "flexible" plate is intended.
2—Clutch shaft bent.
3—Clutch assembly not balanced.
4—Clutch plate does not engage flywheel properly.
5—Backlash in universal joints or propeller shaft whip.
6—Misalignment between engine, clutch, and transmission.

Complete Failure

1—Clutch springs broken or have taken permanent set.
2—Badly worn clutch plate facings.
3—Clutch hub splines sheared.
4—Flexible plate center drive broken.

Faulty Adjustment

1—Unequal spring pressure due to heat or broken springs.
2—Release levers badly bent or worn.
3—Warped or cracked pressure plate.
4—Housing cover bent or broken.

Clutch Sticks

1—Broken, cracked, or split clutch plates.
2—Defective or maladjustment of release bearing.

Indications of Clutch Wear

1—Engine races. Vehicle does not pick up speed.
2—Pedal adjustment used up.

Abnormal or Premature Wear of Clutch Disc Facing

1—Insufficient pedal lash.
2—Driver rides clutch pedal.
3—Excessive slipping of clutch during time of engagement.
4—Abnormal and unnecessary use of clutch.
5—Weak or broken clutch pressure plate springs.
6—Badly warped pressure plate.
7—Use of improper type of friction facing.
8—Friction facing improperly installed.

Uneven Clutch Shaft Spline Wear

1—Misalignment of clutch shaft.
2—Warped clutch housing.

3—Transmission loose on clutch housing.
4—Cracked clutch housing.
5—Frame bent.

Clutch Hub Pulled out of Disc

1—Misalignment of clutch shaft.
2—Transmission loose on clutch housing.
3—Warped clutch housing.
4—Cracked clutch housing.
5—Bent frame.

Weak Springs

1—Excessive heat generated through continual slippage.
2—Overheated springs will show paint burned off or pronounced blue color indicating temper has been drawn. They will also fail to check to specifications.
3—When spring has gray color, temper has been entirely removed.

Grease on Facings

1—Chatter and grabbing when engaged.
2—Slippage at high speed.

Backlash or Bucking

1—Driven member loose on clutch shaft.
2—Pilot bearing worn or broken.
3—*See also* Clutch Noise.

VACUUM CLUTCH CONTROL
Does Not Function Properly

1—Engine idling speed too low. Engine not warmed up. Idle control cam not in hot idle position.
2—Engine misfiring at idling speed.
3—Accelerator linkage binding. Lack of lubrication.
4—Power cylinder piston sticking. Not lubricated.
5—Accelerator and bleeder valve plungers not timed with accelerator throttle in closed position.

Engagement Rough or Jerky with Low Throttle Start

1—Compensator valve closing too late.

Clutch Slips on Low Throttle Start

1—Compensator valve closing too early.

Stalling at Low Throttle Starts

1—Too much lost motion in throttle system. Too much lost motion between accelerator and accelerator valve plunger.

Engagement Rough on Wide Open Throttle Start

1—Cushion control pendulum free movement obstructed. Adjusting screw down too far.

Clutch Slippage on Wide-Open Throttle Start

1—Clutch cushion control pendulum movement too free. Adjusting screw not drawn down far enough.

Clutch Disengages when Driven at Idling Speed

1—Too little lost motion in throttle system. Too little lost motion between accelerator and accelerator valve plunger.

Engine Races when Throttle Is Opened Slightly

1—Piston rod not properly adjusted.
2—Bleeder valve not properly adjusted.

Clutch Engages Too Rapidly

1—Clutch control cable to power cylinder too long.

Clutch Engagement Delayed

1—Clutch control cable to power cylinder too short.

Leakage

1—Piston passes cushion point without hesitation.
2—Leakage around piston rod seal.
3—Leakage at piston packing.
4—Leakage at end plate gasket.
5—Leakage at compensator valve.
6—Leakage at accelerator control valve.
7—Leakage in cushion control.

FLUID FLYWHEEL (CHRYSLER)
Engine Speed Excessive (Similar to Slipping Clutch)

1—Loss of fluid due to leakage.

Leakage

1—Defective gaskets under filler plugs.
2—Loose bolts or defective gasket at crankshaft mounting.

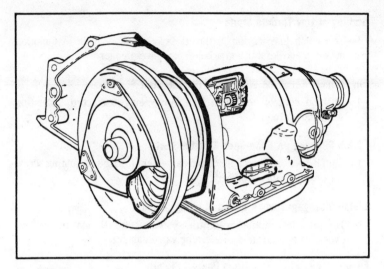

Fluid flywheel.

3—New bellows assembly and seal ring needed if mating surfaces are
scored or show poor contact.

CHASSIS TROUBLES

Chassis noises provide a real problem for the diagnostician because there
are so many contributing sources and conditions to take into consideration.
Noise might appear to originate in the body, but might actually be present in
the power transmission members, the engine or its accessories, or in the
body. It is essential to check all possible sources and the first requisite is to
determine the actual location of the noise before its source can be located.
The following will serve as a guide in analyzing chassis noise.

Squeaks

1—Hood lacing dry or missing.
2—Clutch or brake pedal rubbing on floor board.
3—Brake rods rubbing on adjacent parts.
4—Body not tight against dash.
5—Poorly fitted doors. *See* Body.
6—Loose joints in body framework. *See* Body.
7—Loose tire rim.
8—Loose spokes in wood wheels.

Hood Rattles

1—Poor tension on anti-rattler.
2—Improper adjustment of radiator brace rod.
3—Radiator not properly shimmed.

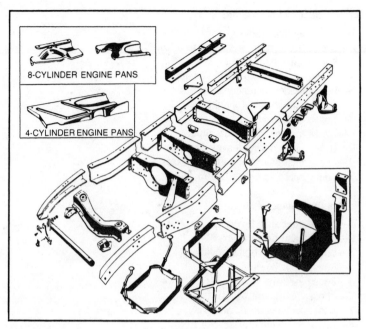

Chassis.

4—Hood riding radiator shell instead of tape.
5—Hood riding cowl instead of tape.

Rattles (Under Front End of Vehicle)

1—Loose headlamps.
2—Loose headlamp doors or lenses.
3—Loose license plates.
4—Loose front apron.
5—Loose radiator shutters or grill.
6—Loose bumper.
7—Improperly fitting hood.
8—Loose radiator or radiator shell.
9—Loose fenders or fender brackets.
10—Loose engine pans.
11—Broken front spring leaves.
12—Loose kick shackle.
13—Loose brake rods or broken support brackets.
14—Loose horn, oil filter, or other accessory.
15—Loose exhaust pipe at engine.
16—Loose radiator to dash brace.
17—Loose steering gear to dash brace.
18—Loose drag link or steering tie-rod.

Rattles (Rear End of Vehicle)

1—Loose bumpers
2—Loose tire carrier or spare tire.
3—Loose gasoline tank.
4—Loose gasoline tank shield or apron.
5—Loose fender or fender brackets.
6—Loose taillight or stoplight.
7—Loose brake rods.
8—Loose muffler or exhaust pipe.
9—Broken rear spring leaves.
10—Loose dust shield or running boards.
11—Loose spare wheel or tire mounting.

Rattles (In or under Vehicle)

1—Loose gear shift lever.
2—Loose hand brake lever.
3—Loose clutch or brake pedal.
4—Loose floor boards.
5—Loose steering wheel.
6—Loose instrument panel.
7—Loose window glass. *See* Body.
8—Loose windshield glass. *See* Body.
9—Loose doors. *See* Body.
10—Loose door window lifts.
11—Loose tools or jack under seats.
12—Loose tools or parts back of upholstery.
13—Loose battery hold-down bolts.
14—Loose brake cross shaft.
15—Worn brake rod clevis pins.

Drumming Noise

1—Loose hood.
2—Loose engine pans.
3—Loose flooring boards.
4—Loose radiator or radiator shell.
5—Loose doors.
6—Loose engine supports.

Bumping Noise

1—Improperly adjusted shock absorbers.
2—Worn spring shackles.
3—Loose body bolts.
4—Broken spring leaves.
5—Battery loose in mounting.
6—Loose steering post.

132

7—Loose tie-rod or drag link.

8—Tools or jack under seat.

9—Knee action (turns on bumpy road at low speed). Wheels out of balance or weak springs in steering connections.

Grating Noise

1—Tight spring shackles.

2—Broken fender brackets.

3—Broken tire rim or loose wheels.

4—Broken spring leaves.

5—Broken dash brackets.

6—Broken radiator stay rods.

Noise Due to Vibration

1—Front wheels out of alignment.

2—Engine loose in frame or rubber mountings improperly adjusted.

3—Transmission or clutch out of alignment.

4—Tight transmission or wheel bearings.

5—Propeller shaft out of alignment.

6—Rear axle out of alignment.

7—Body or sheet metal parts loose.

Dull Thud when Striking Bump

1—Chassis springs too weak or sagged.

2—Chassis springs excessively lubricated.

3—Worn spring shackles or bolts.

4—Radiator loose.

5—Engine mounting loose.

6—Engine cross member loose.

7—Frame sagged or broken.

8—Body loose on frame.

Lost Motion in Power Transmission Line

1—Loose clutch (slipping).

2—Backlash due to wear in transmission.

3—Worn universal joints, worn propeller shaft splines, or loose universal joint flange bolts.

4—Excessive backlash in rear axle gears.

5—Axle shafts loose in differential or wheel hubs.

6—Worn wheel driving dogs or key.

Transmission in Gear, Wheels Do Not Turn

1—Clutch slipping.

2—Axle shaft broken.

3—Wheel hub loose on axle shaft.

4—Wheel bearings broken.

5—Propeller shaft broken.

Misalignment of Frame

1—Unequal braking due to unequalized brakes or variable road adhesion of wheels during braking.

2—Lack of equal wheel traction when accelerating.

Thumping Noise

1—Worn radius rods or bushings.

SPRINGS

Car Rides Hard

1—Excessive tire pressure.

2—Lack of freedom in spring suspension.

3—Improperly adjusted shock absorber.

Squeaks

1—Insufficient lubrication of shackles, bolts, and rebound clips.

2—Corrosion at ends and edges of spring leaves.

3—Frame spring hanger bolt hole worn.

4—Rebound clips too tight.

5—Spring U-bolts loose.

Springs Broken

1—Overloading.

2—Loose spring U-bolts.

3—Center bolt sheared or loose.

4—Defective material.

5—Shackle tension too great locking shackle.

6—Spring seats rusted on axle housing.

Spring Action Stiff

1—Shackles too tight.

2—Shock absorbers improperly adjusted.

3—Wrong springs used.

4—Spring seats on axle too tight.

5—Rust between spring leaves.

6—Spring leaves dry.

Springs Appear to Be Weak

1—Overloading.

2—Overoiling of spring leaves.

3—Wrong springs used.
4—Springs sagged.

Springs Rattle

1—Shackle bolts worn.
2—Shackle bolt holes worn.
3—Frame spring hanger bolt hole worn.
4—Spring hangers loose on frame.

Noisy Spring Shackles

1—Spring shackles or hinge bolts lack lubrication.
2—Spring shackle pins or hinge pins loose in spring ends or in frame brackets.
3—Spring hangers or frame horns loose on frame, bent, or broken.

Spring Shackle Squeaks

1—Lack of lubrication.
2—Tight adjustment.

Shackles Rattle

1—Too much end clearance.

Shackle Bolts Broken

1—Lack of lubrication.
2—Bolts fitted too tight.
3—Spring seats rusted on axle housing.

Center Bolt Sheared

1—Loose spring U-bolts.
2—Broken spring leaf.

SHOCK ABSORBERS
Inefficient Operation

1—Wrong adjustment for driving or climatic conditions.
2—Adjustment disturbed or not equalized on both sides of car.
3—Hydraulic type: low oil level.
4—Friction type: lack of sufficient friction.
5—Spring shackles too loose.
6—Spring shackles too tight.
7—Weak chassis springs.
8—Tires underinflated.

Erratic Ride

1—Roll control bar loose on shock absorber arms.

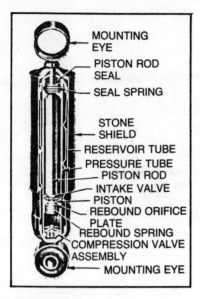

MOUNTING EYE

PISTON ROD SEAL

SEAL SPRING

STONE SHIELD

RESERVOIR TUBE

PRESSURE TUBE

PISTON ROD

INTAKE VALVE

PISTON

REBOUND ORIFICE PLATE

REBOUND SPRING

COMPRESSION VALVE ASSEMBLY

MOUNTING EYE

Shock absorber.

Car Rides Hard

1—Excessive tire pressure.
2—Lack of freedom in spring suspension.
3—Shock absorbers not properly adjusted.
4—Wrong valves or springs in shock absorbers.
5—Stiff spring shackles.
6—Worn spring shackles.
7—Rusted springs.

Shock Absorbers Offer Excessive Resistance

1—Not properly adjusted when adjustable.
2—Calibration changed by replacement of valves.
3—Valve orifice plugged with chips or foreign matter.

Shock Absorbers Lack Control

1—Valves held open by chips or foreign matter.

Shock Absorber Arm Has Free Motion

1—Indicates air is trapped in compression chambers.

Oil Leakage

1—Defective packings or gaskets.
2—Loose or damaged caps or covers.
3—Loose mounting bolts permitting wear resulting in cracked housings.
4—Fluid level too high in housing.

Noisy in Operations

1—Packing washers dry.
2—Link rod anchorage loose.
3—Shock absorber loose on frame.
4—Shock absorber arm striking fender.
5—Shock absorber rubbing on steering connection.
6—Shock absorber striking floor boards.

Squeaks in Operation

1—Rubber insulator distorted. Rubbing on adjacent metal.
2—Packing washers dry.

Squeaking Noise when Stopping

1—Dry shock absorber linkage joints.

Ride Regulator Binds

1—Misalignment of regulator cross-shaft brackets.

UNIVERSAL JOINTS AND PROPELLER SHAFT
Excessive Backlash

1—Improper lubrication resulting in wear and excessive lash between bearing surfaces.
2—Splines on slip joint worn.
3—Loose flange bolts.

Oil Leakage

1—Lubricant plug missing.
2—Oil or grease retainer seals missing or defective.
3—Oil return holes plugged.
4—Overoiling.
5—Use of pressure nipple for lubrication when not permitted.
6—Vent hole in spline shaft plugged.
7—Bearings worn.
8—Excessive vibration of propeller shaft.
9—Clutch grabbing. *See* Clutch.

Propeller Shaft Vibration or Roughness

1—Dry universal joints.
2—Propeller shaft out of balance.
3—Tight torque tube ball.
4—Excessive looseness in torque tube ball.
5—Loose rear spring U-bolts.
6—Loose spring seats on rear axle.
7—Lack of lubrication of clutch parts.

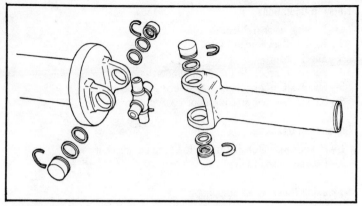

Universal joint and propeller shaft.

8—Dry or sticking clutch release bearing.
9—Glazed clutch plates combined with wear of clutch shaft splines.
10—Wear in bearings of universal joints (open drive).
11—Wear in splines of propeller shaft (open drive).
12—Misalignment of universal joints (open drive).
13—Flange at either end not running true (open drive).
14—Flange at either end loose on shaft; flange bore not contacting shaft (open drive).
15—Flange bent or otherwise damaged (open drive).
16—Spacer between front flange and speedometer drive gear (when used) not square (open drive).

Universal Joints Noisy

1—Misalignment of propeller shaft.
2—Too much play between bearings and journals.
3—Propeller shaft splines worn.
4—Lack of lubrication.
5—Speedometer drive mechanism loose.
6—Propeller shaft bearing in torque tube worn.
7—Disc joint bolts loose. Discs worn.
8—Engine rear supports loose.
9—Engine out of alignment.
10—Cross member rivets loose.
11—Frame sagged, bent, or broken.

Propeller Shaft Broken

1—Lost motion in power transmission line. *See* Chassis.
2—Clutch grabbing severely.
3—Drive pinion loose.
4—Excessive vibration. Any condition causing shaft to whip.

AUTOMATIC CHASSIS LUBRICATION

Tank Lever or Pedal Springs Back Instantly

1—Supply tank empty.

Tank Lever or Pedal Returns Slower than Usual

1—Oil cold or too viscous.
2—Clogged strainer in tank outlet.
3—Wrong kind of oil used in system.

MUFFLER

Vibration

1—Loose mounting bolts or brackets.
2—Loose tail pipe.

Excessive Back Pressure

1—Muffler pipe clogged with carbon.
2—Tail pipe clogged with mud.
3—Tail pipe extending too far into muffler.
4—Strangled outlet at tail pipe.
5—Carburetor heat riser valve stuck.
6—Heat-riser valve broken causing obstruction in exhaust pipe.
7—Muffler replaced; wrong size (not enough capacity).

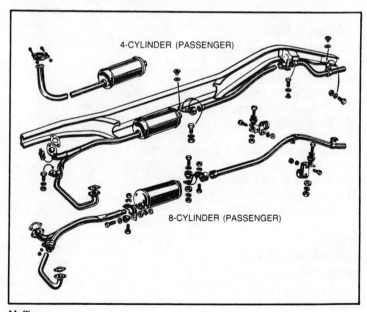

Muffler.

Exhaust Noise

1—Tail pipe extending too far into muffler.

Whistle in Muffler

1—Hole in tail pipe exposed to the rush of air under car.

Rattles

1—Loose mounting bolts or brackets.
2—Loose tail pipe.
3—Loose baffles or tubes.
4—Defective rubber mounting parts.

Leakage

1—Defective packings or gaskets.
2—Split seams in tubing of muffler.

Muffler Burst

1—Fuel charge exploding in muffler. *See* Engine Misfires.

Overheated Exhaust Pipe

1—Spark retarded too far.
2—Strangled exhaust.
3—Clogged muffler.

Explosions in Muffler

1—Spark retarded too far.
2—Weak spark.
3—Engine misfiring.
4—Distributor improperly wired to spark plugs.
5—Weak breaker spring or improper breaker adjustment.
6—Exhaust valve stuck.
7—Mixture too lean.
8—Accumulated unburned gas in muffler.
9—Dirty or sooty muffler.
10—Worn distributor shaft or bearings.
11—Loose connections in ignition wiring.
12—Defective spark plugs.

WHEELS
Front Wheels Loose or Wobbly

1—Wheel bearings loose.
2—Rims out of true.
3—Flange bolts loose.
4—Spokes loose in flange.

Wheel.

5—Wire wheels: unequal spoke adjustment.
6—Steering arm loose.
7—Spindle bolt loose.
8—Spindle bolt or bushings worn.
9—Tie-rod yoke end or bolts worn.

Rear Wheels Loose or Wobbly

1—Spokes loose in flange.
2—Rims not true.
3—Flange bolts loose.
4—Bearings loose or broken.
5—Axle shaft nut loose.
6—Axle shaft bent or broken.

7—Differential bearings loose or broken.

8—Excessive end play in axle shaft.

Squeaking

1—Wheel bearings dry.

2—Rim lugs loose or worn.

3—Spokes loose.

4—Hub flange bolts loose.

5—Felly band loose.

6—Wheel bearings adjusted too tightly.

7—Inner bearings oil seal retainer stuck.

8—Wire wheels: spokes straightened (too short to permit this without noise resulting).

Front Wheel Rattles

1—Bearings too loose.

2—Bearings dry.

3—Bearings tight.

4—Bearings broken.

5—Hub flange loose.

Excessive End Play

1—Excessive wear in axle or wheel bearings.

2—Maladjustment of wheel bearings.

Bearing Noise

1—Bearings too loose or too tight.

2—Bearings dry or broken.

Rear Wheel Bearing Broken

1—Defective bearing retainer.

2—Bent axle shaft.

3—Sprung axle housing.

Bearings Heat

1—Bearings dry or tight.

2—Broken bearing.

Front Wheel Alignment

1—*See* Steering Mechanism.

Rear Wheels Out of Alignment

1—Loose spring U-bolts.

2—Sprung axle housing.

3—Sprung or broken frame.

Wheels Out of Balance

1—Improper tire and tube mounting.
2—Unbalanced tires or misplaced wheel balance lugs.

Wheel Bounce

1—On Chevrolet, rubber bushing at the axle to spring mounting twisted up tight; bolt drawn up before weight is on axle.

REAR AXLE

Axle troubles can be many and varied. The majority of service operations are due to noise. Do not be too positive in assuming that noise always originates in the axle. There are many contributing factors and frequently the origin will be found to be foreign to the axle.

When making replacements, remember that axle gears are ground and mated in sets. Therefore, always replace gears in mated sets. The deter-

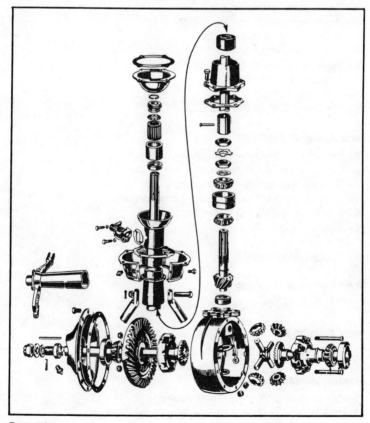

Rear axle.

mining factor in making adjustments is the tooth contact. If the gears are somewhat noisy with proper tooth contact, they will eventually seat themselves and become quiet in operation. Gears that are primarily adjusted for quietness without consideration of tooth contact will eventually fail. The final adjustment must be maintained in operation. Always check and double check to make sure that all bearing adjustments are properly locked so that it will be impossible for them to loosen in service.

Noisy Gears

1—Insufficient or unsuitable lubricant.
2—Improper adjustment of gears and bearings.
3—Gears not mated.
4—Defective gears. Worn teeth.
5—Improper tooth contact.
6—Bevel ring gear warped or broken.
7—Foreign matter at base of tooth space.
8—Pinion shaft bearing broken.
9—Pinion bearing spacers not parallel.
10—Differential gear case broken.
11—Broken differential bearing.
12—Broken differential carrier housing.
13—Sprung axle housing.
14—Vibration caused by tires.
15—Worn axle shaft spacer block.

Noise Foreign to Rear Axle

1—Driving on certain types of pavement.
2—Certain types of tire treads. Use rib treads for test.
3—Transmission or wheel bearing hum.
4—Rear spring seat insulator improperly installed.
5—Muffler or muffler tail pipe vibration.
6—Engine noise.
7—Fan noise.
8—Transmission noise.

Gears Noisy when Coasting

1—Too heavy tooth contact on flank or bottom of ring teeth.

Gears Noisy on Pull

1—Too much backlash between pinion and rear gear teeth.

Growling Differential

1—Maladjustment of pinion shaft bearings.
2—Pinion and ring gear not properly adjusted.

Gear Noise when Decelerating

1—Poor tooth contact of gears.
2—Mismated gears.
3—Lack of backlash between gear teeth.
4—Warped ring gear.
5—Excessive end play in differential bearings.
6—Sprung differential housing.
7—Low tire pressure.
8—*See also* Continuous Axle Hum.

Noisy Axle Bearings

1—Insufficient or unsuitable lubricant.
2—Differential bearings adjusted too tight.
3—Differential or pinion bearings worn.
4—Improper end clearance of axle shaft with center thrust block.

Continuous Axle Hum

1—Faulty lubrication.
2—Differential bearings improperly adjusted.
3—Pinion bearings improperly adjusted.
4—Axle shaft bearings improperly adjusted.
5—Improper ring gear and pinion tooth contact.
6—Ring gear rivets loose.
7—Misalignment of or cracked differential carrier assembly.

Tooth Contact

1—Heel contact indicates too much backlash.
2—Toe contact indicates not enough backlash.
3—Contact at top of tooth pinion out too far.
4—Contact at bottom or flank of tooth. Pinion in too far.

Oil Leakage

1—Oil level too high.
2—Unsuitable lubricant.
3—Oil retainers worn or loose.
4—Bearings worn, broken or loose.
5—Defective gaskets.
6—Frothing lubricant.
7—Defective weld.

Excessive Heating (Melts Lubricant)

1—Sprung axle housing.
2—Sprung pinion shaft.
3—Bent axle shaft.

Excessive Backlash

1—Wheel loose on hub.
2—Wheel hub loose on axle shaft.
3—Too much backlash between ring gear and pinion.
4—Ring gear rivets loose.
5—Spring U-bolts loose.

Differential Gears Stripped

1—Improper lubrication.
2—Foreign matter in lubricant.
3—Improperly hardened gears (remote).
4—Broken differential carrier housing.
5—Broken differential gear case.
6—Failure of bearing locks.
7—Defective or worn bearings.
8—Axle housing sprung.
9—Excessive backlash in power transmission line.
10—Clutch grabbing.
11—Pinion incorrectly adjusted-in too far or out too far.
12—Distorted differential housing.
13—Badly worn differential housing bearings.

Broken Differential Bearings

1—Bearing adjustment too tight.
2—Bevel gear tooth broken.

Rear Wheels Out of Alignment

1—Loose spring U-bolts.
2—Loose wheel bearings.
3—Sprung rear axle housing.
4—Frame or spring broken.
5—Frame bent.

Broken Axle Shaft

1—Loose wheel hub.
2—Poor fit of axle shaft taper in wheel hub.
3—Improper adjustment of wheel bearings.
4—Differential gear case broken.
5—Differential thrust bearings broken.
6—Axle housing sprung.
7—Excessive backlash in power transmission line.
8—Clutch grabbing.
9—Badly worn or unlubricated wheel bearings.
10—Excessive overloading of vehicle.

Broken Axle Housing

1—Overloading of vehicle.
2—Broken gear teeth.
3—Broken differential cage.
4—Foreign matter between gear teeth.
5—Defective weld.

Clink in Wheel at Low Speed

1—Loose pin holding shaft to flange.
2—Loose axle shaft key.
3—Play in driving dogs of full floating axle.

Locked Differential

1—Foreign matter in differential gear teeth.
2—Improper adjustment of bearings.

Snapping Noise

1—Universal joint pins or bushings worn.

Thumping Noise

1—Worn radius rod pins and bushings.

STEERING MECHANISM

Steering troubles demand a complete analysis of the various factors involved in the layout of the mechanism. Quite often these troubles are brought about by a combination of conditions. The solution requires accuracy in checking the various factors. Equipment should be available for this purpose. Consult the specifications covering wheel alignment for the vehicle and make adjustments accordingly.

The average cause of steering trouble can be corrected by applying comparatively simple remedies such as the adjustment of the steering gear and the linkage, properly adjusting the front wheel bearing, replacing worn king pins or knuckle pins and bushings, correction of tire pressure, and wheel balance, and adjustment of toe-in, etc. Much unjustified expense and difficulty can be avoided by checking the small things first.

Steering Wander or Road Weave

1—Unequal tire inflation.
2—Underinflated tires: front or rear.
3—Zero or negative caster.
4—Unequal or too little caster.
5—Insufficient toe-in.
6—Worn knuckle pins or bushings.

7—Worn or loose wheel bearings.
8—Bent steering knuckle.
9—Looseness in steering mechanism.
10—Tight steering mechanism.
11—Tight steering knuckles or ball joints.
12—Lack of lubrication in steering mechanism.
13—Steering gear mast tight or gummy.
14—Spring center bolts sheared.
15—Crosswind.
16—Axle roll on brake application.
17—Reduction too great in steering gear. Also causes oversteering.
18—Bent spindle.
19—Automatic take-up tie rod joints too tight (presenting too much drag).
20—Too little camber.
21—Hudson Auto-Poise Control: torsion bar not centrally located to give equal tension on both sides.

Excessive Amount of Caster
Required to Prevent Car Wander or Road Weave.
1—Tight tie rod joints (especially with self-adjusting type).

Low Speed Shimmy or Wheel Wobble (Under 30 MPH).
1—Tire underinflated or unequal inflation.
2—Unequal or too little caster.
3—Too much caster.
4—Badly worn king pins and bushings.
5—Worn or loose drag link.
6—Worn or loose steering gear parts.
7—Steering gear loose in frame.
8—Front wheel bearing loose.
9—Front wheels out of balance.
10—Tires of unequal weight. Both front tires must be of the same ply.
11—Lack of uniformity in tire threads.
12—Sprung, eccentric, or unbalanced wheels.
13—Improper kick shackle adjustment.
14—Loose or worn front spring shackles.
15—Defective rubber spring shackle.
16—Insufficient shock absorber control.
17—Sprung chassis frame.
18—Weak drag link or steering arms.
19—Bent spindle.
20—Bent or twisted axle.
21—Steering arms loose when bolted to knuckle.
22—Too little camber.

High Speed Shimmy or Wheel Wobble (Above 30 MPH)

1—Any of all of the above conditions.
2—Wheel and tire assembled out of balance.
3—Front springs too flexible.
4—Too much positive caster or camber.
5—Crooked front wheels.
6—Uneven mounting of rim on wheel.
7—Eccentric wheels.
8—Unequal tire pressure.
9—Weak tie-rod.
10—Loose or weak center rubber engine supports.

Steering Kick Back

1—Any or all factors which apply to Low Speed Shimmy.
2—Improper position of steering knuckle ball arm.
3—Weak or sagged front springs destroying steering geometry.
4—Loose spring U-bolts.
5—Improper adjustment of kick shackle.
6—Spring center bolts sheared-axle shifted on springs.
7—Excessive play in steering wheel.
8—Wrong lubricant used in steering gear housing.

Car Pulls to One Side when Applying Brakes

1—Kick shackle adjusted too loose. This allows too much movement of left front spring and causes the car to dive when brakes are applied.
2—Improperly adjusted or unequalized brakes.
3—Loose front spring U-bolts.
4—Insufficient or unequal positive caster.
5—Weak front spring assembly.
6—Improper position of steering ball arm.

Hard Steering (On Road)

1—Wheels out alignment.
2—Tires underinflated.
3—Lack of lubrication.
4—Front wheel bearings too tight or broken.
5—Steering shaft bent.
6—Steering cowl bracket out of alignment.
7—Steering ball connections too tight.
8—Steering spindle arm bent.
9—Steering gear adjusted too tightly.
10—Steering arm bent.
11—Tie-rod bent.
12—Thrust bearings adjusted too tight or broken.

13—Knuckle pins inclined at improper angle.
14—Knuckle pins fitted too tight.
15—Knuckle pin bearings not in alignment.
16—Steering arm rubbing on frame.
17—Excessive caster or front spring sagged.
18—Automatic take-up tie rod joints too tight (presenting too much drag).

Hard Steering (When Parking)

1—Too much caster.
2—Tight or bent spindle.
3—Low or unequal tire pressure.
4—Tight steering assembly.
5—Sagging springs.
6—Automatic take-up tie rod joints too tight presenting too much drag.

Steering Kickback (Road Shock at Steering Hand Wheel)

1—Kick shackle adjusted too tight; does not absorb road shock. Shocks are transmitted to the steering wheel.

Steering Gear Binding

1—Misalignment of steering gear due to installation of body shims. Misalignment of shim steering gear housing to provide proper alignment.

Car Skids on Curve or Turn

1—Speed too high for grade and radius of curve.
2—Smooth tire treads.
3—Tire under-inflated.
4—Condition of pavement.
5—Excessive error in toe-in.
6—Excessive error in steering geometry.
7—Weak chassis springs or shock absorbers.

Loose Steering

1—Loose wheel bearings.
2—Worn king pins or bushings.
3—Loose wheels.
4—Play in steering assembly.

Jerky Steering (More Distant than Shimmy)

1—Bind or play in steering assembly.
2—Misalignment of drag link.
3—Sagging front springs.
4—Bent spindle.
5—Loose wheels.

Wheel Disturbance

1—Loose wheel bearings.
2—Rough bearings.
3—Bent spindle.
4—Loose knuckle pins and bushings.
5—Loose tie rod ends.
6—Bent or twisted wheel.
7—Loose wheel spokes.
8—Front springs too flexible.
9—Shock absorbers not operating.
10—Spring saddles on axle not parallel.
11—Uneven caster.
12—Uneven camber.

Faulty Wheel Camber

1—Wheel spindle bent.
2—Front axle bent.
3—Improper adjustment of wheel bearings.
4—Unequal tire pressure.
5—Knuckle pins or bushings worn.

Rattles

1—Steering gear loose on frame.
2—Steering connecting joints loose.
3—Bushings in steering tube worn.
4—Tie-rod threads worn.
5—Tie-rod yoke ends or bolts worn.
6—Knuckle bushings worn or loose.
7—Steering mechanism worn excessively.
8—Thrust bearings loosely adjusted.
9—Too much end play in steering tube.
10—Spark and throttle quadrant tubes loose.

Steering Gear Loose

1—Steering arm loose.
2—Lateral motion in steering worm shaft.
3—Steering gear loose on frame.
4—Lost motion in drag link.
5—Knuckle bolts or bushings worn.
6—Steering rod ends or bolts worn.
7—Thrust bearings need adjustment.
8—Steering arm shaft nut loose.
9—Thrust bearing broken.
10—Steering mechanism in housing worn.

Rapid Wear of Steering Gear

1—Lack of lubrication.
2—Steering gear improperly adjusted (too tight).

Backlash in Front Wheels (Straight Ahead Position)

1—Improper adjustment of steering gear.
2—Excessive backlash in tie-rod.
3—Excessive backlash in drag link.
4—Loose wheel bearings.

Unequal Movement of Hand Wheel

1—Housing mechanism not centered in making an adjustment.

Loose Knuckle

1—Knuckle pin or bushings worn.
2—Knuckle pin loose.
3—Tie-rod yoke ends or bolts worn.
4—Knuckle arm loose in spindle.

Scuffed or Cupped Tires

1—Improper wheel alignment.
2—Wheels, tires, or brake drums out of balance.
3—Improper camber, worn king pins or bushings.
4—Underinflated tires.
5—Dragging brakes.
6—Improper position of axle on springs.
7—Wheel or tire wobble-runout.
8—Bent wheel spindle, bent, or twisted axle.
9—Steering knuckle bearings worn.
10—Suspension arms bent or twisted.
11—Excessive speed on turns.

INDEPENDENT WHEEL SPRINGING

Steering Wander or Road Weave

1—Unequal or improper tire inflation.
2—Improper wheel toe-in.
3—Improper caster: not equal at both wheels.
4—Improper camber: not equal at both wheels.
5—Knuckle arms bent.
6—Intermediate steering arm bent.
7—Excessive backlash in steering gear.
8—Weak springs in drag link.
9—Play at intermediate steering arm bearing.
10—Play in or frozen drag link joints.

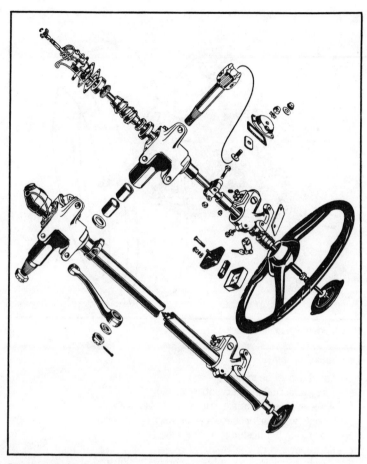

Steering mechanism.

11—Upper or lower support yoke binding due to misalignment.
12—Shock absorbers lack fluid or are improperly adjusted.
13—Improper fore and aft alignment of wheel centers.
14—Axle and frame out of alignment.
15—Rear stabilizer links loose, broken, or bent.
16—Vehicle not the same height on both sides (springs sagged).
17—Loose knuckle arms. Check for sheared keys.
18—Brakes improperly or unevenly adjusted.
19—Wheel bearings adjusted too tight.
20—Rear spring eye straightened out.
21—Steering knuckle arm bent.
22—Crank-arm type: loose support rivets at wheel spindle.
23—Crank-arm type: bent support arm on suspension unit.

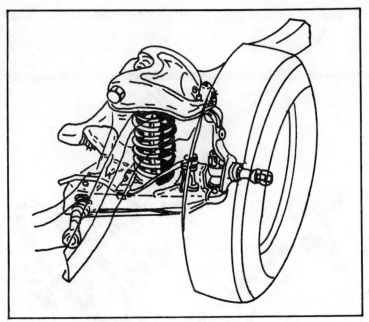

Independent wheel suspension.

Low Speed Shimmy

1—Loose wheel bearings.
2—Tires underinflated, eccentric, or bulged.
3—Wheels, tires, or brake drums out of balance.
4—Excessive wear or looseness in steering linkage.
5—Worn king pin bushings.
6—Improper steering geometry.
7—Shock absorbers unevenly or improperly adjusted.
8—Front springs weak or sagged.

High-Speed Shimmy or Wheel Tramp

1—Unbalanced or improper tire inflation pressure.
2—Wheels and tires not balanced.
3—Blow-out patch on tube (boot in casing).
4—Front wheel bearings not properly adjusted.
5—Wheels eccentric. Runout (max. ⅛″ at rim).
6—Tires eccentric (max. 3/16″ at periphery).
7—Wheel wobble or runout (⅛″ max.).
8—Improper wheel camber or toe-in.
9—Caster not the same at both wheels.
10—Improper king pin angle.

11—Loose king pin and bushings.
12—Steering gear not properly adjusted.
13—Worn bushings in upper and lower control arms.
14—Parts of steering linkage dry.
15—Worn drag link parts.
16—Worn tie-rod parts.
17—Front springs of unequal capacity (unequally compressed).
18—Low fluid level in shock absorbers.
19—Loose rear spring shackles.
20—Crank-arm type: bent front wheel support arm.
21—Crank-arm type: shock absorbers ineffective; check for fluid level, valving, and piston fit.
22—Crank-arm type: noticeable on turns. Bent steering arms permitting wheels to toe-out on turns.
23—Crank-arm type: needle bearings wear ridge in supporting member permitting play on curves.
24—Front-end suspension springs not of equal flexibility or length.
25—Broken front body support bolts.
26—Unbalanced engine, needs tune-up. Engine vibration synchronoized with chassis vibration.
27—Knee action too weak when engine passes through or runs at its cruicial speed.
28—Loose or weak center rubber engine supports.
29—Soft spot in tire or side wall bulge.
30—Unbalanced rear wheel setting up torsional vibration of chassis frame that is being transmitted to front wheels.

Steering Wheel Kickback

1—Tires not properly inflated.
2—Wheels and tires out of balance.
3—Loose front wheel bearings.
4—Worn king pins and bushings.
5—Loose intermediate steering arm bearings.
6—Bent knuckle arms.
7—Bent intermediate steering arm.
8—Loose upper and lower control arm bushings.
9—Improper caster angle.
10—Excessive backlash in steering gear.
11—Broken link or bent arms in suspension system.
12—Broken or weak springs in drag link or tie-rod.
13—Lack of fluid in the shock absorbers or improper operation of shock absorbers.
14—Front springs weak or sagged.
15—Steering knuckle bent.
16—Wrong type or size of tires used.

Erratic Steering on Application of Brakes

1—Low or uneven tire pressure.
2—Brakes improperly adjusted or not equalized.
3—Front springs weak or sagged.
4—Insufficient or uneven caster.
5—Steering knuckle bent.

Thump in Steering Gear

1—Shock absorber bolts connecting arms together near knuckle support are loose.

Squeaks

1—Lack of lubrication.

Lack of Tire Balance

1—Improper assembly of tube, casing, and wheel.
2—Unequal road wear on treads.
3—Blow-out patches on tube.
4—Blow-out boot in casing.

Car Rides Hard

1—Improper tire inflation (pressure too high).
2—Low level of fluid in shock absorbers.
3—Control arm bushings binding.
4—Frozen or dry rear spring shackles.
5—Crank-arm type: brake radius rod binding or bent support arms.

Car Rides Too Soft

1—Tires underinflated.
2—Improper shock absorber fluid level.
3—Shock absorbers not properly adjusted.

Excessive Front Tire Wear

1—All factors listed under High-Speed Shimmy or Wheel Tramp must be eliminated.
2—Wrong type of tire used.
3—Wheels and tires not concentric.
4—Wheel runout excessive.
5—Steering knuckle arms, supports, or frame bent.
6—Frame out of alignment.
7—Rear axle out of alignment.

Cross Scuffing of Front Tires

1—Unequal toe-in on opposite wheels.

2—Unequal caster with weight on tires.

3—Variation in front wheel tread due to misalignment.

Excessive Rear Tire Wear

1—Check conditions under Steering Wander or Road Weave.

2—Excessive runout of tires (max. ⅛″).

3—Rear axle housing out of alignment.

Loss of King Pin Bearing Plug

1—Use of high pressure or power grease gun. Use hand pressure gun only.

Transmissions and Gear Shifts

TRANSMISSION

Slippage of Free-Wheel Unit

1—Wrong oil being used for seasonal temperatures.

Noise in Free-Wheel Unit

1—Backlash in members which lock unit.

Inefficient Operation of Unit

1—Replacement of parts which are not matched.

Inefficient with Free-Wheel Unit Locked Out

1—Excessive end play in free-wheeling unit drive shaft.

Failure to Synchronize

1—Incomplete clutch release.

2—Lubricant too heavy for seasonal temperatures.

3—Clogged oil holes to bearings of gears.

4—Dirt in transmission.

5—Parts not operating freely.

6—Gears bind on splined shaft.

7—Incorrect end play in cam sleeve.

8—Shifter forks loose.

9—Improper operation of shifter forks.

10—Worn thrust washers permitting too much end play.

11—Plunger spring tampered with.

12—Sliding sleeve torn.

13—Broken plunger ball.

14—Clogged oil groove in synchronizing cones.

15—Nicks or burrs on steel or bronze cones.

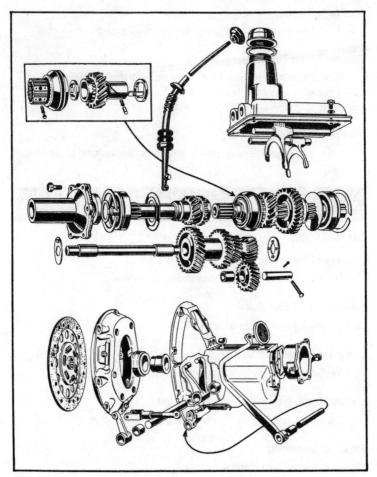

Transmission.

Transmission Noisy

1—Insufficient or unsuitable lubricant.
2—Misalignment of clutch and transmission.
3—Dirt in transmission bearings.
4—Gears not meshed properly.
5—Main drive gear worn.
6—Idler gear loose on shaft.
7—Countershaft bearings worn or broken.
8—Constant mesh gears not mated.
9—Worn bearings destroying alignment of gears.
10—Metal chip wedged in tooth of one gear.
11—Gear striking adjacent teeth (excessive end play).

12—Damaged or worn gears.
13—Bent clutch splined shaft.
14—Bent transmission shaft.
15—Transmission case broken.
16—Clashing of gears. Too much end play.
17—Broken spring on gear shift lever plunger.
18—Gear shift lever plunger worn.
19—Engine torsional periods being transmitted to transmission.
20—Clutch plate damper inoperative or improperly adjusted.
21—Clutch plate damper springs weak or broken.
22—Rear main shaft bearing worn, rough, or dirty.
23—Excessive end play in unit.
24—Noisy speedometer gears.

Noise at High Speed

1—Lack of balance of rotating parts such as universal joints, propeller shaft, and clutch.
2—Universal joints not in alignment.
3—Worn rear transmission rear bearings permitting propeller shaft to whip.
4—Universal joints worn excessively.
5—Miaslignment of clutch and transmission.
6—Bent clutch shaft.

Noise Except on High Speed

1—Lack of lubrication.
2—Sliding gears worn.
3—Rear main shaft pilot bushing or bearing worn.
4—Main drive gear worn.
5—Main drive gear bearing worn.
6—Countershaft gears worn.
7—Countershaft bearings worn or broken.

Grating or Grinding Noise

1—Damaged or broken insulation disc in clutch.
2—Unsuitable lubricant.
3—Gears not properly meshed.
4—Sliding gears worn.
5—Bearings worn or broken.
6—Main drive gear broken.
7—Countershaft gears worn.
8—Reverse idler gear seized.

Howl at Low Speed

1—Misalignment of clutch in flywheel.

2—Binding of clutch hub on splined shaft.
3—Defective clutch pilot bearing.

Noise in Reverse

1—Reverse gears worn.
2—Reverse idler bushing worn.
3—Reverse idler gear loose in case.

Noise in Neutral

1—Insufficient or unsuitable lubricant.
2—Constant mesh gears not mated to marking.
3—Excessive end play in transmission.
4—Main shaft pilot bushing worn.
5—Excessive wear of countershaft and reverse idler bushings.
6—Lack of end play in synchro-mesh unit.

Noise when Disengaging Gears

1—Low or reverse: damage to pointing on side of countershaft gear, reverse idler, or low-speed gear.
2—Both low and reverse: fault in low-speed gear only.
3—On reverse only: fault in countershaft gear only.

Clashing of Gears (Noisy Gear Shifting)

1—Clutch pedal not properly adjusted. Clutch does not release fully.
2—Dragging clutch.
3—Clutch release binding on shaft.
4—Heavy oil in clutch (oil-type clutch).
5—Broken clutch disc.
6—Bent shifter forks.
7—Bearings worn.
8—Countershaft gears loose.
9—Excessive end play in countershaft.

Rattles

1—Gears loose on splines.
2—Sliding gears grating on countershaft.
3—Shifter shaft worn.
4—Main drive shaft worn.
5—Main drive gear bearing rough.
6—Front splined shaft bearing broken or worn.
7—Countershaft bushings worn, rough, or broken.
8—Idler gear loose on shaft.
9—At high speed, improper clutch driven plate damping.
10—At low speed or part throttle, improperly calibrated driven plates or scored axle gears.
11—Defective engine torsional balancer.

Gears Jump Out of Mesh

1—Gears not meshing properly.
2—Worn sliding gears.
3—Misalignment of clutch and transmission.
4—Bent shifting forks.
5—Shifter forks not properly aligned.
6—Lost motion in shifting parts.
7—Lock plunger spring weak.
8—Lock plungers worn.
9—Loose or sprung clutch plate.
10—Bent clutch shaft.
11—Sprung flywheel housing.
12—Bent transmission shaft.
13—Main drive gear worn.
14—Worn transmission bearing.
15—Warped transmission housing.
16—Misalignment of free-wheel cable control.
17—Worn parts in free-wheel unit.
18—Rear wheels not tracking with front wheels.
19—Bearing locks in transmission loose or broken permitting excessive end play.
20—Vibration or propeller shaft whip due to wear in universal joints.
21—Propeller shaft out of balance or bent.
22—Misalignment due to defect in or too flexible rear engine mounting.
23—Worn clutch pilot bearing or sprung clutch shaft.

Gears Jump Out of Mesh (High Gears)

1—Misalignment of clutch and transmission with flywheel.
2—Excessive main shaft end play.
3—Damaged or poor fit of sliding sleeve or synchronizing unit in clutch gear.
4—Loose bearings or bushings.
5—Improper tension on shifter rail springs.

Gears Jump Out of Mesh (Second Gear)

1—Poor or damaged fit of sliding sleeve on synchronizing unit in second speed gear.
2—Fit of sliding sleeve or synchronizing unit on main shaft too loose.
3—Excessive main shaft end play.
4—Worn bearings or bushings.
5—Improper tension on shifter rail springs.

Gears Jump Out of Mesh (Low Speed or Reverse)

1—Fit of sliding sleeve and main shaft and low speed gear too loose on main shaft.

2—Loose bearings or bushings.

3—Improper tension on shifter rail springs.

Hard Gear Shifting

1—Bent or sprung shifter forks.

2—Nicks or burrs on gear teeth.

3—Too much tension on shifter rail springs.

4—Scored synchronizing cones or drums.

5—Rough cam surfaces on ends of sliding sleeve.

6—Rough synchronizing cones or drums.

7—Excessively tight fit of low and reverse sliding gear and synchronizer assembly on main shaft.

8—Paint or lack of lubrication on gear shift lever ball.

9—Rough gear shift lever ball.

10—*See also* Clutch.

Oil Leakage

1—Too much oil in transmission case.

2—Cover gaskets defective.

3—Loose, defective, or missing gaskets.

4—Damaged oil throw ring.

5—Reverse idler shaft turning in case.

6—Shifter shafts worn.

7—Broken or cracked transmission case.

8—Damaged or improperly installed oil seals.

9—Housing plugs loose or threads damaged.

10—Shift lever oil seal damaged or improperly installed.

11—Use of lubricant that foams excessively.

Excessive Backlash

1—Excessive play between clutch gear and high-speed sliding gear.

2—Sliding gears loose on splines.

3—Main shaft bearings worn or broken.

4—Main shaft pilot bearings worn, broken, or loose.

Squeaks

1—Dry or hard oil seal at rear end of unit.

Fails to Function

1—Unsuitable lubricant.

2—Improperly assembled.

3—Dirt or grit in unit.

4—Cams of synchro-mesh unit not assembled in proper relation.

Overheating

1—Insufficient supply of lubricant.
2—Excessive use of transmission hand brake on long grades.

Oil Leakage to Rear Axle (Torque Tube Drive)

1—Scored universal joint or bushing.
2—Plugged drain from torque tube ball.
3—Excessive clearance in bushing.
4—Loose adjustment of ball parts.
5—Runout at end of propeller shaft.

AUTOMATIC TRANSMISSION (BUICK AND OLDSMOBILE)

Shift lever will move between low and high range torque on.

1—Misalignment of detents at shift lever boss and in transmission.

Excessive vibration on accelerator pedal accompanied by a loud chatter or rattle in transmission. Most likely to occur in low range or possibly in third gear at high speed.

1—Low oil lever causing oil pump cavitation.

Slight vibration on accelerator pedal accompanied by a light buzzing sound.

1—Pressure regulator valve buzz. Noticeable only when oil is cold. Annoying but not serious.

Transmission fails to manually shift from high to low range, with oil cold, or shift is delayed for a reasonable interval.

1—Drag of cold oil on manual control valve.

Transmission will not down shift from fourth to third or it requires excessive accelerator pedal pressure to make this shift.

1—Improperly adjusted throttle control lever.
2—Throttle control rod is adjusted too long.

Down shift fourth to third occurs before increased resistance in accelerator pedal travel is felt.

1—Improperly adjusted throttle control lever.
2—Throttle control rod is adjusted too short.

Car fails to move in low or reverse gear.

1—Improperly adjusted servo brake band.

Transmission fails to shift out of low gear with shift lever in either high or low range.

1—No oil in transmission.
2—Pressure regulator valve tight in body.
3—Oil pump not working.
4—Bad oil leak inside of transmission.

Transmission shifts rapidly and violently between first and third gear at low speeds after prolonged driving at high speed.

1—Oil in transmission might be too light for temperature and service to which transmission has been subjected.

Shift from first to third gear very severe and bumpy after car is broken in.

1—Improper throttle control lever adjustment.

2—Defective or worn clutch plates.

Shift from first to third gear accompanied by slipping within the transmission if the pressure down shift (third to first) is below 4 mph. Hot oil.

1—Improper throttle lever adjustment.

2—Defective or worn clutch plates.

Shift from first to third gear accompanied by slipping within the transmission, if the pressure down shift (third to first) is too high—approximately 8 to 10 mph. A severe hunting or rapid shifting between first and third usually accompanies this trouble.

1—A bad oil leak in the transmission causing the oil pressure to drop when car speed is too high.

No automatic shift from first to second or third to fourth gear.

1—High unit or automatic valve not working properly.

2—Valve might be sticking.

3—Stop pin out.

4—Bind in governor linkage.

5—Faulty or defective governor.

Automatic upshift or downshift occuring at speeds too high or too low. Shift erratic.

1—Governor out of adjustment.

Oil pump and governor drive gears badly worn or loose on shaft.

1—Improper end clearance in oil pump body. Outer drive gear serrated; not on shaft far enough and when pump is tightened to case, the outer drive gear strikes the bracket and forces the assembly out against the pump cover. This will increase the driving load on the pump.

SAFETY GEAR SHIFT (PONTIAC)

Improper Adjustment

1—Shift lever not horizontal in neutral. Eccentric stud in transmission not properly adjusted.

2—Shift lever too close to steering wheel. Cable not properly adjusted.

3—Shift lever too far from steering wheel. Cable not properly adjusted.

4—Too much lost motion at lever pivot. Shims required to remove excessive clearance.

5—Too much travel when shifting. Looseness in eccentric ball stud. Riveted ball on lever stud loose or loose nut on transmission cover shift shaft.

6—Shift lever shakes when driving over rough roads. End plugs in control rod loose. Anti-rattle spring in upper support not in place. Cover shift shaft not free or plug in lower end of control rod adjusted too tightly.

7—Shift lever sticks from low to high speed side. Selector plate does not move freely. Pin binds in notches of selector plate. Warpage of selector plate due to improper assembly of cover. Selector plate out of line.

Kink in control cable. Lock nuts on cable loose or shift lever binding at its pivot.

8—Too much travel when selecting. Control cable nuts in transmission may be loose.

9—Shift lever hits steering column jacket. Eccentric ball stud not properly adjusted.

10—Lower lever hits jacket when shifting. Eccentric ball stud not properly adjusted.

11—Spring tension too light or too heavy when selecting. Improper adjustment of control cable nuts.

Noise in Mechanism

1—Rattle at lever pivot. Rod shims required to remove excessive clearance.

2—Buzz at inner end of lever-tension spring and plunger not in place or not seating on gear shift lever ball.

3—Rattle in shift shaft. Rubber sleeve not located at middle or missing.

4—Buzz or rattle in lower end of shift shaft. Anti-rattle spring not in place.

5—Control rod rattles or clicks when shifting. End plugs not properly adjusted or ball seats not in place.

6—Selector plate or shift bar rattles. Flat anti-rattle spring not in place on selector plate retainer.

7—Rattle under toe board on rough road. Selector control cable rattling against speedometer cable.

EVANS VACUUM GEAR SHIFT

Graham, Nash, and Studebaker.

Gear Shift Fails to Operate

1—Leaks in intake manifold or at connections to valve and cylinder.

2—Faulty assembly or adjustment of linkage between cylinder and gear shift lever.

3—Control valve not centered due to maladjustment. Air not admitted to front or rear of cylinder as required for shift.

4—Air cleaner located at control valve clogged.

5—Piston rod binding in its bearing.

6—Control valve rod binding in valve.

7—Linkage between unit and dash requires lubrication.

8—Shifter rails binding in transmission cover.

CHEVROLET VACUUM GEAR SHIFT

Sticky Shift when Selecting Gears

1—Check for free action of lever. Disconnect selector control rod from selector lever and check up and down movement of lever if lever does not return freely to the downward position.

2—Binding of pivot pins in control shaft bracket.
3—Clearance between gear shift lever in bracket.
4—Roughness or burrs in bracket.
5—Rubber anti-rattle bushing on selector binding in control shaft.
6—Binding of the selector lever bell crank in lower support assembly.
7—Clearance between the upper face of selector control lever guide and end of control shaft.
8—Bent selector control rod causing binding in selector control lever.
9—Check movement of selector lever on transmission.

Hard Shift

1—Hard shifting in all gears. Check for leak in vacuum line and its connections.
2—Hard shifting into high gear only. Check position of vacuum hose clamp at cylinder for interference with speedometer cable. Check tightness of screws in the control shaft lower support.

Creeping Out of Gear

1—Check position of vacuum hose clamp at cylinder for interference.
2—Check reactionary lever and shifting linkage for binding and lubrication.
3—If above does not correct trouble, replacement of vacuum cylinder is necessary.

Blocking Out of Gear

1—Selector rod bent, (making it too long). Replace.
2—Control lever not moving forward far enough. Check assembly limits of steering column unit.
3—Cylinder vacuum hose clamp interference.

Excessive Lash in Gear Shift Lever

1—Looseness of shift control lever on control shaft. Clamp bolt must be pulled down hard to lock lever firmly to shaft.

ELECTRIC HAND

Failure to Function

1—Open circuit from ignition switch to circuit breaker.
2—Defective selector switch or switch wiring.
3—Leakage in vacuum connections or units.
4—Cutout switch on selector housing not "on."
5—Loose connections at junction block.
6—Solenoid connections loose in steering column jack.
7—Broken wires or damaged insulation.
8—Defective circuit breaker.

Shift Made with Clutch Engaged

1—Circuit breaker makes contact with too little clutch pedal travel.
2—Short circuit in clutch circuit breaker.
3—Improper timing of circuit breaker arm.

Gears Butt (Shift Not Complete)

1—Too much clutch pedal travel required to make circuit breaker contact.

Gear Shifting Retarded Excessively

1—Transmission lubricant too viscous (especially in cold weather). Replace 3 ounces of lubricant with kerosene.

Short Circuit

1—With instrument panel lamp lighted, shift into all positions with Electric Hand. Any appreciable dimming of instrument lamp indicates a short circuit in that position.

Current Normal, but Shift Not Made

1—Valve plunger sticking in upward position.
2—Vacuum leakage in lines or units.
3—Mechanical drag in mechanism.

Current Draw of Solenoid Excessive

1—Solenoid short circuited.

Current Draw of Solenoid Low

1—Solenoid open-circuited.

Diaphragm Cylinder Does Not Function when Disconnected

1—Power unit defective. Replace.

Shifting Cylinder Does Not Function when Disconnected

1—Power unit defective. Replace.

Bearings, Tires, and Body

ANTIFRICTION BEARING DEFECTS: ROLLER BEARINGS

Pitted Cup

1—Improper lubrication.
2—Improper adjustment.

Overloaded Bearing

1—Cone and roller assembly forced on shaft that is too large.
2—Cone or cup not started and seated squarely.

Chipped Rollers (At Large End)

1—Adjustment too tight. Too little end play (.005″ practically standard).

Chipped Rollers (At Small End)

1—Adjustment too loose. Too much end play.

BALL BEARINGS

Stick when Spun

1—Presence of tiny particles of metal or dirt wedged between balls and races.

Failure Due to Overloading

1—Misalignment.
2—Cocked bearing in mounting.
3—Fit or adjustment too tight.

Note: Failure is generally indicated by "flaked" balls, "pitted" races, or both.

Failure Due to Lapping

1—Abrasive material in lubricant.

Worn Loose, Not Flaked or Pitted

1—Dirty lubricant.

Failure Due to Locking

1—Damage to balls and races by large particles of foreign matter in lubricant (causing balls to wedge in races).

TIRES

Excessive Wear of Front Tires

1—Underinflated.
2—Unequalized brakes.
3—Faulty wheel alignment.
4—Worn or loose wheel bearings.
5—Bent tie-rod or knuckle arm.
6—Worn knuckle pin or bushing.
7—Bent or sprung front axle.
8—Reckless brake application.
9—Steering arms loose when not integral with knuckles.

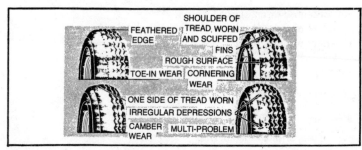

Tires.

Excessive Wear of Rear Tires

1—Underinflated.
2—Brakes grabbing or reckless application.
3—Unequalized brakes.
4—Loose spring U-bolts.
5—Pinion or ring gear broken.
6—Sprung rear axle housing.

Tires Do Not Run True

1—Wheels out of true.
2—Rims not trued up on wheels.
3—Axle not square with frame.
4—Springs of unequal length.
5—Frame sprung or bent.

Bruised

1—Excessive flexing of side wall due to underinflation.
2—Rim bruise due to curb scraping.
3—Casing run flat on rim.

Excessive Tread Wear

1—Underinflation.
2—Unequalized brakes.
3—Faulty wheel alignment.

Cupping of Front Tires

1—Low tire pressure.
2—Incorrect wheel toe-in.
3—Improper camber.
4—Too much or too little caster.
5—Spring center bolt sheared.
6—Improper steering geometry.
7—Dragging brakes.

8—Eccentric or unbalanced wheels.
9—Bent or twisted axle.
10—Bent wheel spindle.

Jumping

1—Improper mounting on rim.

Wobbling

1—Improper mounting on rim.

Tube Chaffing

1—Improper mounting on rim.

Scuffing

1—Under-inflation.
2—Improper toe-in or camber.
3—Bent spindle.
4—Bent or twisted axle.

Squeal or Howl

1—Flexing of side walls in turning corners.
2—With proper inflation and front wheel alignment. Evidence of turn being taken too fast.

Distinct Whistle or Squeal when Rounding a Curve

1—Lateral slippage or side drag of front tires due to misalignment of front wheels.

Tire Noise

1—Irregular tread wear.
2—Underinflation.
3—Foreign material wedged in tread.
4—Trapping of air between tread projections due to tread design.

Car Rides Hard

1—Excessive tire pressure.

BODY

Squeaks

1—Door dovetails not functioning properly.
2—Tight door hinge pins.
3—Loose halves of hinges.
4—Lack of lubrication of door latch and striker plate.

170

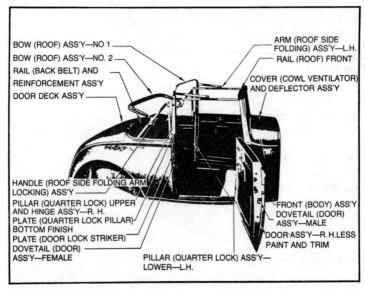

BOW (ROOF) ASS'Y—NO 1

BOW (ROOF) ASS'Y—NO. 2

RAIL (BACK BELT) AND
REINFORCEMENT ASS'Y

DOOR DECK ASS'Y

ARM (ROOF SIDE
FOLDING) ASS'Y—L.H.

RAIL (ROOF) FRONT

COVER (COWL VENTILATOR)
AND DEFLECTOR ASS'Y

HANDLE (ROOF SIDE FOLDING ARM
LOCKING) ASS'Y

PILLAR (QUARTER LOCK) UPPER
AND HINGE ASS'Y—R. H.

PLATE (QUARTER LOCK PILLAR)
BOTTOM FINISH

PLATE (DOOR LOCK STRIKER)

DOVETAIL (DOOR)
ASS'Y—FEMALE

FRONT (BODY) ASS'Y

DOVETAIL (DOOR)
ASS'Y—MALE

DOOR·ASS'Y—R.H.LESS
PAINT AND TRIM

PILLAR (QUARTER LOCK) ASS'Y—
LOWER—L.H.

Automobile body.

5—Door rubbing on pillar lock.

6—Metal panel rubbing at flanges.

7—Loose moulding at front pillar.

8—Body weaving causing floor board chafing.

9—Tight fitting floor boards.

10—Body riding dust shield.

11—Friction between cowl panel and body sill.

12—Loose side panel nails in sills.

13—Noisy cushion or back springs.

Rumbles

1—Loose window or windshield glass.

2—Loose door or body panels.

3—Vibration of door and body panels.

Scraping or Cracking Noise

1—Loose moulding at front pillars.

2—Loose front pillar corner.

3—Friction between metal panel and roof moulding.

4—Chafing of roof slats or bows.

Door and Hinge Squeaks

1—Loose hinge screws or bolts.

2—Dry or tight hinge pins.

171

3—Door metal panel rubbing on hinge at flange cutaway.
4—High spots in body panels at door flanges.

Door Rattles

1—Worn rubber bumpers.
2—Lock bolt chafing on striker plate.
3—Lock bolt loose in lock facing.
4—Loose striker plate due to excessive pressure on door bumpers.
5—Worn striker plate.
6—Wear at back of door latch.
7—Loose hinge screws or bolts.
8—Worn door check.
9—Excessive clearance at door check link.
10—Poor contact or lack of lubrication of dovetail parts.
11—Door metal loose on hinge post.

Noise at Lock Bolt

1—Striker plate worn.
2—Loose bolt lock facing.
3—Bolt well at striker plate not deep enough.

Window Rumbles

1—Garnish mouldings improperly adjusted to glass run channels.
2—Glass does not fit to full depth of channel opening (allowing glass to move sideways).
3—Loose window panels.
4—Panel nails loose.
5—Metal rubbing on frame rivets.

Regulator Rattle

1—With windows down, too much play in the regulator parts.
2—End play in glass.

Windshield Rattle

1—Excessive play and vibration.
2—Glass loose at garnish mouldings.
3—Windshield mounting loose.

Door Check Squeak

1—Lack of lubrication.
2—Lack of clearance.
3—Misaligned check.

Noise at Shroud or Belt Moulding

1—Loose body bolts.
2—Shims absent or insufficient at front body hold-down bolts.

Cowl Ventilator Noise

1—Wear in ventilator assembly mounting and control parts.

Noise at Sill and Sash

1—Loose body bolts.
2—Too little shimming under body.

Roof Noise

1—Chafing of roof slats or bows.

Hood Rattles

1—Insufficient tension on hood fastener.
2—Anti-rattlers defective or missing.

Door Misalignment

1—Improper shimming of body to align door with door openings.
2—Door sprung.
3—Improper action of door side bumpers.

Doors Bind

1—Sprung hinges.
2—Loose door hinges.
3—Dry hinges-rusty hinge pins.
4—Worn hinge pins.
5—Misalignment of door wedge plate.
6—Body hold-down bolts loose.
7—Misalignment of body on chassis.
8—Door lock handles improperly lubricated. Might become stiff acting.

Regulator Slips; Glass Does Not Raise

1—Teeth or gear worn or stripped.
2—Sash channels pulled off glass.

Regulator Binds

1—Lack of lubrication.
2—Side garnish moulding too tight against glass run channel.
3—Glass binding in run channel.
4—Glass and channel moving with window.
5—Glass does not fit properly.

Glass Breakage

1—Improper adjustment of garnish moulding.
2—Glass not lined up in run channel.
3—Metal retainer in door panel misaligned.
4—Glass contacting on metal or tacks or window header strip.
5—Improper door action. Dry hinges or inoperative door bumpers.

Leakage at Back Window

1—Imbedding putty works loose.

Leakage at Top of Door

1—Roof drip moulding does not fit against top material.

Leakage at Door Window Sash Weather Strip

1—Water drains at door panel clogged.
2—Window sash channel not locking against sash rubber weather strip.

Leakage at Windshield

1—Improper adjustment of windshield regulator board adjusting screws.
2—Weather strip at glass too thick.
3—Glass not seating on weather strip.
4—Joint at bottom corners of windshield not properly filled with compound.

Leakage at Shroud or Belt Moulding

1—Front of body not properly aligned.
2—Insufficient shim under front body bolt.

Door Lock Does Not Operate Properly

1—Dirt working into key slot.
2—External plunger or shank damaged.
3—Internal plungers do not function.
4—Key too far or not all the way in slot.
5—Key turned too far or not far enough.

Shock Received when Touching Body Hardware

1—Tires generating static discharged through body. Paint tire rims with three coats of aluminum paint as an insulator.
2—Generator not properly grounded.
3—Poor engine ground.
4—Static discharge through lack of brake lining clearance.
5—Static caused by friction of airstream on body.
6—Body not grounded to frame of car.

Index